SPORTSMAN'S DIGEST

of FISHING

ABOUT THE AUTHOR

Hal Sharp was just four years old in 1918 when
his great-grandfather took him on a squirrel hunt
in the Ozark Mountains of north-west Arkansas,
and he has been hunting ever since. Hal was
initiated, too, into the secrets of angling with
a "trot" line at the age of four.

When he was nine, he moved with his family to
California where he attended school and won a
three-year scholarship in art. Later he worked in
the animation studios at Hollywood and for three
years was a comic book illustrator.

During the Second World War, Hal was a technical
engineer and did radar installation drawings for the
U. S. Navy. It was at this period in his career
that he decided to create the newspaper feature,
SPORTSMAN'S DIGEST [from which this book was
compiled], to help other sportsmen learn short cuts
to the art of hunting and fishing that otherwise
might take years of learning.

Nowadays when Hal hits the road with gun or rod,
he takes his wife along.

SPORTSMAN'S
DIGEST
OF FISHING

BY HAL SHARP

BARNES & NOBLE, Inc., New York

Booksellers • Publishers • Since 1873

Reprinted, 1971

L. C. catalogue card number: 54-5727

SBN 389 00244 5

Printed in the United States of America

TABLE OF CONTENTS

SPORTSMAN'S DIGEST
OF FISHING

THE SPORT
OF FISHING

Angling is the most popular of all American sports. Anglers spend about four times the amount spent by spectators and participants of all other outdoor activities—combined — including baseball, football, basketball, racing and track, but excluding hunting which ranks second to fishing.

If you are interested in learning all you can about angling, keep your mind, eyes and ears open and you will observe much that would otherwise pass you by. Be friendly but don't ask too many questions or act like a know-it-all. The locals will resent your presence and you will be the loser. You can't force anyone to tip you off if he doesn't like you. Some of the finest anglers

1

will spend hours observing a new location before planning their own strategy. They study the stream, the anglers, and how they are fishing.

Some of the tips in this book may be "as old as the hills" to you, but you may be reading others for the first time. There are little tricks to every trade. Some of these are closely guarded "secrets" discovered after years of experimentation or given to me by friendly fishermen.

In some areas some fishing methods are illegal but the same methods are legal and popular in other regions. Therefore, every angler should learn the fishing laws of every area he fishes in. It is not my purpose to show you how to beat the law. It is best to support your local laws whether you are caught or not, because the laws were designed to protect your future supply of fish.

Fishing is one of man's oldest pursuits. Cave dwellers of France recorded such activities with drawings on their cave walls some 15,000 years ago. Picture records also show that the ancient Egyptians fished with rod and line as early as 2,000 to 3,500 B.C. Artificial lures were first recorded in writing about the year 200 B.C.

One of the primitive techniques, still practiced in some places today, might well have been "noodling" or "cuddling." This consists of quietly approaching the fish and stroking its belly gently with the fingers to lull it into a sleep-like trance and then gently lifting it out of the water before it regains its senses. Don't attempt this! A "noodler" who sticks his fist into a big catfish's mouth to aid in capturing it may lose his battle if the fish closes its jaws and the hand cannot be withdrawn. A big 40- to 100-pound catfish can be a dangerous opponent. He can pull a husky man into the depths of a pool under such circumstances, and has done it!

The use of artificial flies was first described in a book entitled "The Boke of St. Albans" by a certain Dame Juliana Berners of England, printed in 1486. It later served as the basis of another book, "The Compleat Angler" by Izaak Walton (whom many regard as the first angling authority). Walton was a successful retired linen draper when his book was published in 1653, almost 200 years after Dame Juliana's.

An angler who fishes dry flies exclusively is referred to as a "purist" by other anglers. If the "purist" is a snob he refers to anglers using different methods as "meat hunters" and "nonsportsmen." Some "purists" begin by fishing with bait and later change to dry flies. Other "purists" who try a different technique sometimes become converts to the other method. Methods differ, but the sport is the same regardless of what techniques you apply.

All fishing can be fun. Of course you want to catch fish as well as enjoy the scenery and fresh air. Sometimes you will go home empty-handed, and other times you may catch fish in spite of yourself when everything is contrary to the rules. In any event, if you are a real angler, you will be back again the first chance you have to try your luck.

Luck frequently enters into one's fishing success, but knowledge of fish habitats and habits, of streams and of handling equipment and bait are more important than luck. Learn all you can about fish and perfect your casting ability. Join rod and gun clubs and read everything you can upon the subject. You may not agree with all this author has to say, but chances are you will learn a few important things anyway.

All fishing has one basic idea: you are trying to deceive a fish into taking your lure whether it is an artificial or live bait. Don't be afraid to try a technique usually reserved for other fish.

Trout are frequently taken by bass-finding methods and vice-versa.

Bear in mind that not all waters contain fish. You must learn the favored haunts of the fish, so keep a record or notes of just where you caught fish, in what type of water, and what conditions prevailed, and you will build up a great fund of angling knowledge. Good luck and good fishing!

TOPOGRAPHIC MAPS ARE VERY HELPFUL!

Sᴄᴀʟᴇᴅ ½" TO 2" PER MILE THE...

MAPS ARE VERY ACCURATE IN ALL DETAIL, SHOWING STREAMS, ROADS, HILLS, ETC. WRITE THE GEOLOGICAL SURVEY, WASHINGTON, D.C., FOR A FREE INDEX OF THE STATE OR TERRITORY DESIRED. THE INDEX LISTS THE QUADRANGLES AVAILABLE FOR A FEW CENTS EACH TO COVER COSTS. IN CANADA, SURVEYS & ENGINEERING BR., DEPT. MINES & RESOURCES, OTTAWA.

6

CHARTS OF LAKES

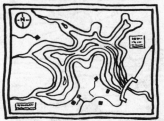

IT IS NEC-
ESSARY TO
KNOW A
LAKE'S
BOTTOM
STRUCTURE,
LOCATION
OF CHANNELS, SAND BARS,
WEED BEDS, VARIOUS DEPTHS,
ETCETERA TO FISH IT BEST.
CHARTS OF SOME LAKES ARE
AVAILABLE WHICH ARE A GREAT
HELP IN FISHING SUCH WATERS
FOR THE FIRST TIME UNLESS A
RELIABLE GUIDE IS HIRED. LO-
CAL TACKLE STORES OR LAKE
OFFICIALS MAY SUPPLY CHARTS
OR SOURCES THEREOF IF THE
LAKE HAS BEEN
CHARTED.

PARTS OF A LARGE
LAKE MAY OFFER
POOR SPORT YET
BE EXCELLENT
ELSEWHERE. A
CHART WILL
HELP.

GRAND LAKE

WHEN DO FISH FEED?

THE OBVIOUS ANSWER IS WHEN THEY ARE HUNGRY. DIGESTION IS SLOW WHEN WATER TEMPERATURE IS LOW AND FISH ARE INACTIVE. AS WATER WARMS, DIGESTION SPEEDS UP AND FISH MAY FEED MORE THAN ONCE EVERY DAY IF TEMPERATURE IS IDEAL, ALTHOUGH MANY ANGLERS WRONGLY THINK SUCH FISH FEED ONLY ONCE A WEEK! IN COOLER WATER, FISH DEEP. IN WARMEST WATER, FISH DEEP OR IN SHADE.

IDEAL WATER TEMPERATURES FOR POPULAR FISH ARE: TROUT, ABOUT 50° TO 70° F.; LAKE TROUT, 35° TO 48° F.; SMALLMOUTH BASS, 58° TO 70° F.; LARGEMOUTH BASS, 60° TO 90° F.; WALLEYES, 55° TO 70° F.; MUSKY, PIKE AND PANFISH, 60° TO 80° F.

THE BEST FISHING DEPTHS IN SUMMER

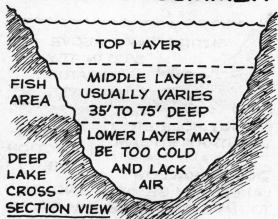

TOP LAYER

MIDDLE LAYER.
USUALLY VARIES
35' TO 75' DEEP

FISH
AREA

LOWER LAYER MAY
BE TOO COLD
AND LACK
AIR

DEEP
LAKE
CROSS-
SECTION VIEW

WHEN THE SUN WARMS THE TOP LAYER ABOVE 39.2° IT BECOMES LIGHTER IN WEIGHT THAN THE COLD WATER BELOW, SO IT STAYS ABOVE AND THE STAGNATION REMAINS UNTIL FALL'S TURNOVER. THE MIDDLE DIVIDING LAYER VARIES IN DEPTH WITH LAKE SIZE AND DEPTH. THIS AREA OF RAPID TEMPERATURE DROP HAS THE BEST COMBINATION OF TEMPERATURE AND OXYGEN, SO COLDWATER FISH FEED NEAR THE BOTTOM WITHIN THIS LAYER.

SUMMER FISHING IN SHALLOW LAKES

Chapter 1

Locating
the Best
Fishing

ENTIRE LAKE ABOVE
39.2° IN TEM-
PERATURE

COLD
SPRING HOLE OR
TRIBUTARY STREAM

(CROSS-
SECTION
VIEW)

SOME SHALLOW LAKES MAY BE DEEP ENOUGH TO HAVE AREAS BELOW 39.2° IN TEMPERATURE WHERE COLD-WATER FISH FEED ON THE BOTTOM. SHALLOWER LAKES WILL HAVE NO COLD-WATER FISH IN TEMPERATURES ABOVE 39.2° UNLESS THERE ARE COLD SPRING HOLES OR TRIBUTARY STREAMS FOR THEM. SUCH INLETS USUALLY SUPPLY THE BEST FISHING AS SHOWN ABOVE.

WARM WATER WITHOUT COLD INLETS IS SUITABLE TO LARGE-MOUTH BASS, WALLEYES, PICKEREL AND PANFISH. AT 55° TO 60° BASS FEED BEST FROM 10:00 A.M. TO 4:00 P.M. BETWEEN 5 AND 10 FT. DEEP UNDER WEEDS, ETC.

10

FINDING THE RIGHT FISHING DEPTH.....

MANY ANGLERS FISH AT DIFFERENT LEVELS UNTIL A CATCH INDICATES THE FEEDING LEVEL BUT IF FISH AREN'T FEEDING, IT BECOMES HEARTLESS!

IF YOU LEARN THE FISHES' PREFERRED WATER TEMPERATURES YOU'LL SAVE TIME BY TAKING WATER TEMPERATURE AT 5 FT. INTERVALS UNTIL THE RIGHT LEVEL IS FOUND. THUS, YOU KNOW HOW DEEP TO FISH AT THE START. FISH JUST ABOVE THE BOTTOM AT THAT DEPTH!

11

SURFACE WATER TEMPERATURES FOR BEST FISHING

Here are the fishes' preferred WATER temperatures. When SURFACE water is in this temperature range in AUTUMN'S COOLING PROCESS, shallow fishing is best.

Ideal water temperatures in Fahrenheit are: Brook trout, 58°; rainbow and brown trout, 61° to 68° (67° for dry flies); smallmouth bass, 67°; largemouth bass, 60° to 73° although they have hit bugs up to 89°; lake trout, 41°; salmon, 45°; pickerel, northern pike, muskellunge and pan fish, 60° to 80° and walleyes, 55° to 70°. Trout & salmon may vary by 10°.

LOCATING THE FISH

UNLESS YOU KNOW A STREAM'S BEST FISH HIDE-OUTS, IT WILL PAY YOU TO MAKE A SILENT APPROACH WITH THE SUN AT YOUR BACK. WHEN CLOSE ENOUGH TO SEE THE BOTTOM, THROW YOUR SHADOW ACROSS THE WATER. IF THAT DOESN'T SCARE THE FISH, STAMP THE BANK OR TOSS A FEW STONES IN THE WATER. SOMETIMES YOU WON'T SEE THE FISH BUT YOU MAY SEE HIS DEPARTING WAKE. RETURN LATER OR NEXT DAY WITH CAUTION TO FISH WHERE THE QUIETED FISH HAVE RETURNED TO THEIR FAVORITE HIDE-OUTS.

WHERE YOU CATCH A FISH IN A CHOICE HIDING PLACE, ANOTHER FISH WILL TAKE ITS POSITION SO FISH IT ON LATER TRIPS.

STALKING THE FISH

IMPROVE YOUR CHANCES OF CATCHING FISH BY CAREFULLY KEEPING LOW AS YOU APPROACH A FISHING SPOT. MOVE SLOWLY, AS IF YOU'RE PART OF THE SCENERY. FISH AREN'T WARY OF INACTIVE SILHOUETTES. AVOID CASTING A SHADOW BUT KEEP THE SUN TO YOUR BACK SO ITS RAYS ARE NOT REFLECTED FROM YOU TO THE FISH AS SHOWN.

WRONG

POOL FISHING TIP

WHEN A BAIT FISHERMAN LOCATES SEVERAL SMALL FISH IN A POOL, HE CAN CATCH MORE THAN ONE IF HE CONCEALS HIM- SELF WHERE HOOKED FISH CAN BE FLIPPED OUT EASILY. OTHER FISH MAY FOLLOW THE FIGHT SO SHORTEN IT TO AVOID ALARM. QUICKLY SKID FISH TOWARD YOU AND FLIP IT OUT.

IF THE FISH IS TOO BIG TO FLIP OUT, YOU DON'T MIND SHOWING YOURSELF TO ALARM THE OTHERS.

15

THE QUIET HOLDS IN SWIFT WATERS

QUIET WATER CUSHION

A CUSHION OF QUIET WATER SURROUNDS A ROCK IN THE PATH OF A CURRENT. FISH HOVER ALMOST AT REST IN THESE HOLDS, EVEN IN SWIFT CURRENTS.

A STREAM'S MAIN CURRENT CARRIES MOST OF THE FISHES' UNDERWATER FOOD BUT IF FISH HAD TO FIGHT THIS CURRENT CONTINUOUSLY WITHOUT REST THEY WOULD SOON TIRE. INSTEAD, WHEN THEY SEE A MORSEL COMING BY THEY DART OUT, GRAB IT AND RETURN TO THESE QUIET HOLDS.

16

WARNING THE FISH BY VIBRATIONS...

SOUND VIBRATIONS CREATED BY CARELESS WADING IN ROCKY STREAMS RADIATE MANY FEET AWAY TO WARN THE FISH EVEN THOUGH IT CAN'T SEE THE CAUSE WHICH SCARES HIM AWAY!

BOAT FISHERMEN MUST USE CARE NOT TO DROP OR BANG ARTICLES IN A BOAT, WHETHER THE WATER IS ROUGH OR NOT, WHEN APPROACHING AN AREA

THE PROPER
BAIT-CASTING TACKLE

You do not need the most expensive tackle to begin fishing, but it might aid in casting. On the other hand, an expensive bamboo rod's action can easily be damaged by a beginner and it may lose its "backbone" as a result. Therefore, it's best to learn casting with a suitable but cheaper bamboo or glass rod.

An inexpensive nylon line is good to start with. Buy this one size larger than a line of silk for the same rod. Silk casts the best but it's more expensive to learn with.

In other tackle buy the best you can afford. It will last longer and you need never blame the tackle for a lack of fishing success. Provide yourself with tackle that suits the water and species of fish you are angling for.

Buy sparingly of lures to begin with. They all look tempting but it's easy to buy more than you need to start.

DOES YOUR CASTING ROD FIT YOU ?

HEAVY-MUSCLED MEN CAN USUALLY CAST BEST WITH A SHORT, MEDIUM-LIGHT ACTION ROD BECAUSE THEY USE MORE MUSCLE IN CASTING. SLIGHTER-BUILT PERSONS NEED ADDED LEVERAGE OF LONGER, LIGHT ACTION RODS TO AVOID FATIGUE AND FORCING THEIR CASTS.

WEIGHT OF THE LURES SHOULD FIT THE ROD ALSO. USE AN EXTRA-LIGHT ACTION, 5½- TO 6-FT. ROD FOR ¼-OZ. LURES, A 5- TO 5½-FT., LIGHT-ACTION ROD FOR

ADD LENGTH TO ROD IF YOU ARE OF SLIGHT BUILD!

⅜- TO ½-OZ. LURES AND A 5-FT., MEDIUM OR 4½-FT. LIGHT-ACTION ROD FOR ⅝-OZ. LURES. CONSIDER THESE SIZES WITH YOUR BUILD.

SELECTING A BAIT CASTING REEL

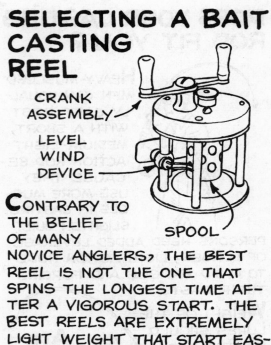

CRANK ASSEMBLY

LEVEL WIND DEVICE

SPOOL

CONTRARY TO THE BELIEF OF MANY NOVICE ANGLERS, THE BEST REEL IS NOT THE ONE THAT SPINS THE LONGEST TIME AFTER A VIGOROUS START. THE BEST REELS ARE EXTREMELY LIGHT WEIGHT THAT START EASILY AND SLOW UP QUICKLY, ONCE THE IMPELLING FORCE IS STOPPED. A HEAVY SPOOL AND GEARS OF CRANK ASSEMBLY AND LEVEL WIND CREATE A DRAG AT THE START OF A CAST BUT THE SPEED SOON OVERTAKES THE FLOWING

LINE SPOOL (END VIEW)

LINE TO REVERSE IT ON THE SPOOL, CREATING THE "BACKLASH" Ⓐ AND A POOR CAST!

IMPROVE DISTANCE WITH CASTING REELS

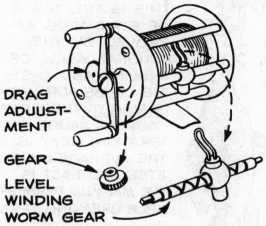

DRAG ADJUST-MENT

GEAR

LEVEL WINDING WORM GEAR

DRAG ADJUSTMENT TENSION, USED TO HELP PREVENT BACK-LASH OF LINE IN BAIT CASTING, MAY BE GRADUALLY RELEASED IN A DAY'S FISHING AS THUMB CONTROL BECOMES MASTERED. WHEN YOU CAN CAST WITHOUT THIS TENSION, STILL MORE DIS-TANCE IS ACHIEVED BY TAKING OFF THE LEVEL-WINDING WORM GEAR AND ANY EXCESS GEARS THAT DRAG IN CASTING. YOU CAN LEARN TO WIND LINE IN FAIRLY EVEN. USE LIGHT WEIGHT REELS AND THE LIGHTEST, REASONABLE WEIGHT LINE AS WELL.

SIZE AND BREAKING TEST OF LEADERS

THIS IS THE TABLE OF STANDARDS APPROVED BY THE NATIONAL ASSN. OF ANGLING AND CASTING CLUBS FOR <u>NATURAL GUT</u>. THE FIRST FIGURE IS GAUGE DESIGNATION, NEXT IS THE AVERAGE DIAMETER AND LAST IS THE MINIMUM PERMISSIBLE BREAKING TEST.

			7X − .004½ − ¼		
			6X − .005 − ⅜		
5X − .005½ −	½	8/5 − .013 − 3½
4X − .006 −	⅝	7/5 − .014 − 4
3X − .007 −	¾	6/5 − .015 − 4¾
2X − .008 −	1	5/5 − .016 − 5½
1X − .009 −	1½	4/5 − .017 − 6¼
0X − .010 −	2	3/5 − .018 − 7½
10/5 − .011 −	2½	2/5 − .019 − 8¾
9/5 − .012 −	3	1/5 − .020 − 10

NYLON TESTS AS FOLLOWS:

DIAM.	TEST	DIAM.	TEST
.012 −	4	.019 −	12
.014 −	6	.021 −	15
.015 −	8	.023 −	20
.017 −	10		

BOBBERS WITH LESS ALARM HELP YOU TO CATCH MORE FISH!

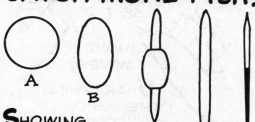

A   B   C   D   E

SHOWING FIVE BASIC TYPES RANGING UP TO EXCELLENT WITH TYPE E IN PERFORMANCE. MORE PULL IS NECESSARY TO SUBMERGE A THAN E, THE LATTER IS A SOUTH AMERICAN PORCUPINE QUILL (HARD TO GET IN NORTH AMERICA). QUILLS FROM NORTHERN SPECIES, OF LESSER AIR CAPACITY, ARE UNSUITABLE.

A TESTING FISH MAY REJECT THE BAIT IF IT RESISTS. IF NOT, HE GRABS AND SWIMS AWAY WITH IT.

YELLOW PERCH

23

USE SHARP HOOKS

(HONE
MOVES)

Sharpening
THE INSIDE OF
THE POINT WITH
A HOOK HONE

Many fish are missed
BEING HOOKED BECAUSE OF
A DULL OR DAMAGED HOOK.
EVERY TIME A HOOK IS SNAG-
GED IT SHOULD BE INSPECTED.
EACH FISH HOOKED DULLS THE
POINT. NEEDLE-SHARP, A HOOK
IS MORE EASILY SET AND FEW-
ER STRIKES ARE MISSED.

Showing HOW TO HONE THE
HOOK SIDES.

(HOOK
MOVES)

FISH HOOKS FOR A SPECIFIC FISH......

SNECK

SNECK HOOK IS FOR SOFT MOUTHED FISH SUCH AS SUCKER, CARP, WHITEFISH AND CRAPPIE. WEAK HOOK, NOT TOO POPULAR.

SPROAT HOOK IS A LATER VERSION OF THE SNECK. IN HEAVIER WIRE, IS POPULAR FOR STEELHEAD AND SALMON.

SPROAT

EAGLE CLAW

EAGLE **C**LAW HOOK IS A NEW DESIGN. IT IS POPULAR FOR ALL BAIT FISHING TYPES. MADE IN VARIOUS LENGTHS AND THICKNESS. Ⓧ SHOWS BAIT HOLDER, SLICED SHANK.

CARLISLE HOOK IS FOR SUCKING OR GULPERS SUCH AS SUCKERS, SUNFISH PERCH, FLOUNDER, ETC. LONG SHANK AIDS IN REMOVING HOOK.

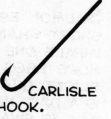

CARLISLE

THE RIGHT HOOKS
FOR BEST RESULTS

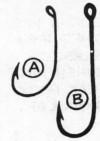

SMALL DIAMETER WIRE IS PREFERRED FOR TROUT AND BASS HOOKS WITH A CLAW BEND PATTERN AS SHOWN IN Ⓐ. THE FINER WIRE WILL NOT TEAR WORMS AS EASILY AS HEAVIER WIRE, THUS A LARGER SIZED HOOK MAY BE USED. THIS TYPE IS SUITABLE FOR ALL SOFT MOUTHED FISH. USE A LONGER SHANK HOOK FOR SUCKERS.

HARD MOUTHED PIKE, PICKEREL, MUSKIES, ETC. REQUIRE A HEAVIER WIRE HOOK WITH A LONGER SHANK SUCH AS A CARLISLE TYPE Ⓑ HAVING A PLAIN RINGED EYE.

SALMON EGG HOOK IS SHORT-SHANKED TO IMPALE ONE OR MORE EGGS ON IT. SLICED SHANK Ⓒ IS A BAIT HOLDER. EGG IS SWALLOWED.

EGG

26

POLISHED SPOONS CATCH MORE FISH

RUB BACK AND FORTH ⊗ IN ONE DIRECTION FOR A SHINY FINISH TO...

...POLISH ALL METAL FINISHES. CIRCULAR OR CRISS-CROSS MOTION PRODUCES A DULL FINISH.

USE SILVER POLISH FOR GOLD, SILVER AND CHROME PLATED SPOONS. SOLID COPPER OR BRASS SPOONS DULL MORE QUICKLY IN SOME WATERS. USE FINE STEEL WOOL FOR THESE SPOONS THAT MAY NEED RUBBING SEVERAL TIMES A DAY.

IT'S THE <u>SHINE</u> THAT ATTRACTS!

CLEAR LACQUER OR SPAR VARNISH PROTECTS THE FINISH!

27

BASS BUG TIPS...

A POPULAR TYPE OF CORK BODY BUG THAT FLOATS. SELECT 3 OR 4 DIFFERENT COLOR BUGS TO VARY IN USE SUCH AS BLACK, BROWN, RED AND YELLOW OR WHITE. IF ONE DOESN'T WORK, SWITCH COLOR. THEY ALL PRODUCE.

POPPER BASS BUGS ARE VERY POPULAR IN MANY SIZES AND COLORS. THE SMALL SIZES TAKE PAN FISH, TROUT, BASS AND OTHER GAME FISH.

PAINT CHIPPED AND CRACKED SPOTS WITH FINGER NAIL POLISH ONLY WHEN BUG IS ABSOLUTELY DRY. BUGS SO TREATED WILL FLOAT MUCH BETTER.

REPAINT YOUR OLD BATTERED BAIT-CASTING PLUGS!

RED FINGERNAIL
POLISH
(OR LACQUER)

WHITE OR
YELLOW

WINTER IS A GOOD
TIME TO REPAINT
OLD PLUGS THAT ARE
CHIPPED AND SCARRED.
ARTIFICIAL EYES AND
LACQUER ARE OFFERED BY SUPPLY
HOUSES. THE COST IS REASONABLE.

RED AND WHITE (OR YELLOW) IS
AN IDEAL COMBINATION. IT IS
EFFECTIVE ON ALL TYPES OF
PLUGS. IT'S EASIER TO PAINT
THE HEAD OF ONE PIECE PLUGS
BY USING A STRIP OF SCOTCH
TAPE FOR A GUIDE.

TAPE

29

BAIT-CASTING TIPS

Bait-casting, perhaps the most popular fishing method, is an art it will pay you to learn. Most fishermen learn about angling by using bait. A fly fisherman can learn much about using artificials by first using live bait. Authorities usually agree that live bait will most consistently attract the largest fish.

Plugs and spoons are a "natural" to use with a bait-casting rod and reel. Don't expect to catch fish the first time you use them, because this, too, is an art that takes study and practice. Most users of plugs work their lures too fast. Take it easy! If a fish doesn't strike it as soon as it hits the water, let it lay awhile before beginning the retrieve. Then reel in very slowly, pausing now and then. You never see a frog racing across the water. Vary the retrieves as much as you can but try to make your plugs act like something that belongs there by nature or as an accident! Work the plug like the thing it imitates.

CORRECT BAIT CASTING GRIP CASTS A GREATER DISTANCE!

GRASP THE GRIP SO THAT THE REEL HANDLES POINT UPWARD WHEN THE ARM IS EXTENDED (AS WOULD BE

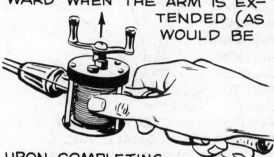

UPON COMPLETING A CAST). THIS WILL PERMIT A BETTER BALANCE WITH A VERTICAL SUPPORT FOR THE SPOOL AND HANDLES, RESULTING IN GREATER DISTANCE.

RELAX, DON'T FORCE CAST!

31

BAIT CASTING FORM

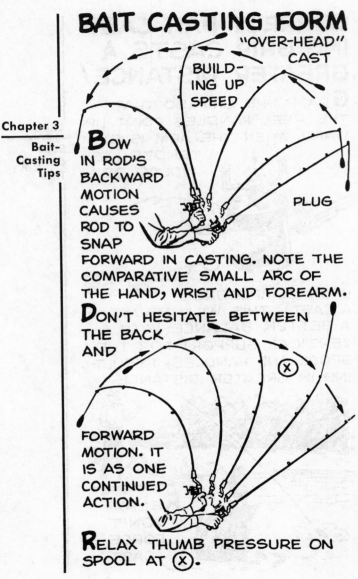

"OVER-HEAD" CAST

BUILD-ING UP SPEED

PLUG

BOW IN ROD'S BACKWARD MOTION CAUSES ROD TO SNAP FORWARD IN CASTING. NOTE THE COMPARATIVE SMALL ARC OF THE HAND, WRIST AND FOREARM.

DON'T HESITATE BETWEEN THE BACK AND FORWARD MOTION. IT IS AS ONE CONTINUED ACTION.

RELAX THUMB PRESSURE ON SPOOL AT ⊗.

32

ANTI-BACKLASH TIPS FOR BAIT CASTING

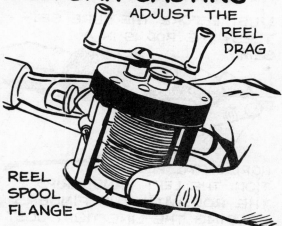

ADJUST THE REEL DRAG

REEL SPOOL FLANGE

THUMB MAINTAINS A SLIGHT CONTACT ON FLANGE (OR SPOOL, AS SOME PREFER) WHILE THE LURE IS IN FLIGHT, "FEELING-IT-OUT," AND FOR BRAKING THE FLIGHT OF THE LURE. POINT THE ROD AT THE LURE IN ITS FLIGHT TO REDUCE LINE DRAG ON THE GUIDES. WHEN THE SPEED OF THE REEL'S SPOOL OUTRUNS THE PULLING OF THE LINE IT BACKLASHES THE LINE.

33

USING BOTH HANDS IN BAIT CASTING....

JUST BEFORE THE LURE SETTLES, THE ROD IS IN A SEMI-

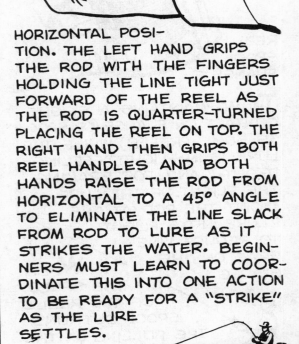

HORIZONTAL POSITION. THE LEFT HAND GRIPS THE ROD WITH THE FINGERS HOLDING THE LINE TIGHT JUST FORWARD OF THE REEL AS THE ROD IS QUARTER-TURNED PLACING THE REEL ON TOP. THE RIGHT HAND THEN GRIPS BOTH REEL HANDLES AND BOTH HANDS RAISE THE ROD FROM HORIZONTAL TO A 45° ANGLE TO ELIMINATE THE LINE SLACK FROM ROD TO LURE AS IT STRIKES THE WATER. BEGINNERS MUST LEARN TO COORDINATE THIS INTO ONE ACTION TO BE READY FOR A "STRIKE" AS THE LURE SETTLES.

ACCURATE PLUG CASTING CATCHES MORE FISH

USE A RUBBER PRACTICE PLUG SUCH AS TOURNAMENT CHAMPIONS DO, OR FILL A SMALL TOBACCO SACK WITH SAND TO TIE ON THE LINE. PRACTICE CASTING AT A BUSHEL BASKET OR OLD TIRE A FEW MINUTES EACH DAY IN THE YARD.

BEFORE EACH CAST, LINE UP THE ROD TIP WITH THE TARGET. TRY THUMB PRESSING THE REEL TO STOP THE PLUG DIRECTLY OVER THE TARGET SO THAT THE PLUG DROPS IN IT.

THE SIDE CAST FOR WINDY WEATHER

PLUG OR BAIT CASTING INTO A HEAD WIND USUALLY RESULTS WITH LESS DISTANCE AND SO IN STRAINING TO IMPROVE DISTANCE, A BACKLASH (NEST-LIKE SNARL OF LINE ON THE REEL) IS THE REWARD!

YOU CAN CAST FARTHER IF YOU KEEP THE CAST LINE AND LURE LOW. THIS CALLS FOR THE SIDE CAST SHOWN ABOVE. IT IS NOT AS ACCURATE AS THE OVER-HEAD CAST BUT IT WILL SERVE.

BE CAREFUL OF ALL BYSTANDERS!

FISH GETTING TIPS

AIM YOUR CAST A FOOT OR TWO IN THE AIR OVER THE WATER SO THAT IT SEEMS TO HOVER BE-FORE IT SETTLES. THIS WILL NOT ALARM THE WAITING FISH AS MUCH AS A LURE WHICH GOES BOUNCING OVER THE WATER.

GIVE INTEREST TO A LURE BY CHANGING FROM FAST TO SLOW RETRIEVES AND VICE VERSA. GIVE IT A JERK AND LET IT LAY FOR A BIT, THEN JERK IT AGAIN, ETC.

RETRIEVE TRICKS

PAUSE

IMITATING
ALARMED
ESCAPE

WHEN FISH REPEATEDLY FOLLOW YOUR LURE WITHOUT STRIKING, TRY THIS:

STOP THE RETRIEVE SHORT OF COMPLETION, BEFORE FISH SEES YOU. PAUSE A MOMENT THEN RAISE ROD AND RETRIEVE FAST. THIS IMITATES SUDDEN AWARENESS OF PURSUIT FOLLOWED BY A DESPERATE ESCAPE ATTEMPT OF YOUR LURE.

SKIDDING A LURE ON THE SURFACE IMITATES A SMALL FOOD FISH CHASED THERE BY FEEDING GAME FISH BELOW. TRY IT FOR VARIETY WHEN SLOW RETRIEVES FAIL.

WORM RIG FOR HIGH, ROILY WATER

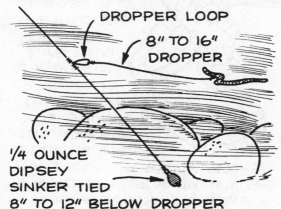

DROPPER LOOP

8" TO 16" DROPPER

¼ OUNCE DIPSEY SINKER TIED 8" TO 12" BELOW DROPPER

USE MONOFILAMENT NYLON IN MAKING THIS RIG. USE DIPSEY TO SINK WORM DEEP WHERE FISH HUG THE BOTTOM. IF THE SINKER SNAGS EASILY IN ROCKS, TIE SINKER TO A WEAKER DROPPER AND PUT WORM WHERE THE SINKER WAS. THUS, ONLY THE SINKER IS LOST WHEN SNAGED, SAVING BAIT AND HOOKS. IF THE WATER IS VERY MUDDY, TIE A SMALL INDIANA SPINNER 6" ABOVE THE WORM AS AN ATTRACTOR.

SINKING BAITS....

IT'S BEST TO AVOID USING SINKERS WITH BAIT WHENEVER POSSIBLE. WHEN BOAT FISHING FOR BASS OR PANFISH, 2 LARGE NIGHTCRAWLERS WITHOUT SINKERS MAY WORK BETTER THAN 1 WORM AND SINKER. IT'S IDEAL WITH A FLY ROD.

BOTTOM-TYPE MINNOWS SUCH AS SUCKERS TEND TO GO DEEP WHEN USED FOR BAIT. UNLESS WATER IS QUITE DEEP OR FAST, THEY MAY NOT NEED SINKERS. OTHER MINNOWS THAT STAY NEAR THE SURFACE NEED SINKERS IN FISHING DEEP.

A MUD BALL FORMED AROUND BAITED HOOK DISOLVES AFTER SINKING. TOSS IT OUT BY HAND.

FISH THE BOTTOM!

WHEN OTHER METHODS HAVE FAILED TRY THIS BOTTOM TRICK!

BASS AND WALLEYES GO FOR THIS AS WELL AS SALT WATER FISH SUCH AS WEAKFISH, SNOOK AND TARPON. SOME FISHERMEN USE THIS METHOD EXCLUSIVELY FOR THE LATTER!

USE A SPOON AND PORK RIND (THE FIRST CHOICE) OR SINKING PLUG. LET IT SINK. LET IT LIE FOR VARYING PERIODS THEN JERK IT UP. THEN RELAX AGAIN TO REPEAT. IT IMITATES A WOUNDED FISH!

STILL-FISHING WITH A LIVE FROG.......

CHECK
LOCAL LAWS
ON USING
FROGS!

Lacking a frog harness, a frog may be hooked through the upper or lower hind leg.

For surface fishing, use a greased (to float) nylon line and a sinking leader without sinkers so frog swims freely. Drop frog overboard from a boat and move 100 ft. away to anchor, paying line as you go to leave frog behind. After a strike, give fish time to get frog well into his maw before setting hook. If you don't get a strike in 30 minutes, pull anchor and drift to another location.

42

FORCING NIBBLERS TO STRIKE HARD!

FISH WILL OFTEN LIGHTLY NIBBLE THE END OF A WORM. THE GENTLE TUGS CEASE OR YOU STRIKE TO FIND MOST OF THE WORM GONE BUT NO FISH! SOMETIMES IT PAYS TO SLOWLY PULL THE WORM AWAY FROM THE TEASER AND THIS MAKES HIM STRIKE IT HARD. THEN YOU GIVE THE LINE A TUG TO SET THE HOOK. IT DOESN'T ALWAYS WORK BUT IT IS WORTH TRYING.

WHEN TO STRIKE IN BAIT FISHING WITH WORMS

IF A FISH GRABS HARD AND BEGINS A FAST RUN DOWN-STREAM, DON'T FEED HIM LINE BUT STRIKE AT ONCE. OTHER-WISE HE WILL FEEL

THE ABRUPT CHECK OF THE LINE (YOU CAN'T PAY IT OUT AS FAST AS HE CAN SWIM), AND HE'LL SPIT IT OUT!

WHEN THE TUGS ARE UNCERTAIN, WAIT UNTIL THEY FEEL SOLID. WITH EXPERIENCE YOU LEARN THE FEEL OF THESE THROBS. SLOWLY AND GENTLY TAKE UP SLACK LINE UNTIL THE PULL IS AS DIRECT AS POSSIBLE FROM THE HOOK TO THE ROD. NOW THE THROBS ARE SOLID SO <u>STRIKE</u> AT ONCE!

44

REMOVE BELLY IN A LINE BEFORE YOU SET THE HOOK....

WHEN BAIT FISHING
FOR SPECIES
THAT. . .

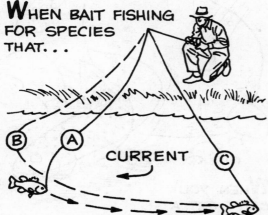

CURRENT

...MOUTH THE BAIT BEFORE
TAKING IT SOLIDLY, A DELAY IN
STRIKING RANGING FROM A FEW
SECONDS TO SEVERAL MINUTES
IS NECESSARY. IN A STREAM, A
BELLY IN THE LINE ⒷFORMS IN
A FEW SECONDS IF SLACK IS
PAID OUT TO FISH MOVING UP-
STREAM FROM Ⓐ TO Ⓒ. THIS
BELLY-DRAG WARNS SUSPICIOUS
FISH TO LET GO AND MAKES A
STRIKE DIFFICULT. INSTEAD, TRY
TO KEEP A TAUT LINE Ⓒ WITH A
SLIGHT PRESSURE (DON'T WARN
FISH!) TO BE READY TO STRIKE.

45

STIRRING UP FISH

WHEN YOU CAN'T GET A HOOKED FISH TO MOVE FROM BEHIND A ROCK AFTER STRUMMING THE LINE OR TAPPING THE ROD, TRY THROWING STONES AT HIS LOCATION. THIS WILL OFTEN CAUSE HIM TO MOVE AWAY SO THAT YOU CAN PLAY HIM WITHOUT BREAKING YOUR LINE IN PULLING. BE CAREFUL NOT TO HIT YOUR FISHING LINE OR LEADER, HOWEVER.

EVEN THOUGH TROUT MAY NOT TAKE SPOONS CAST ALL AROUND A LAKE, IT MAY WAKE THEM UP SO THEY WILL TAKE A WET FLY!

46

HOW TO PLAY A FISH

WHEN A LARGE FISH FIGHTS TOWARD A HEAVY GROWTH OF WEEDS, BRUSH, ETC., IT IS TRYING TO FIND LEVERAGE TO BREAK AWAY. MANY GOOD FISH ARE LOST THIS WAY, SO APPLY MORE ROD PRESSURE AND THUMB THE REEL SPOOL HARDER TO FORCE THE FISH TO CHANGE ITS DIRECTION.

REEL IN LINE WHENEVER IT'S POSSIBLE BUT DON'T FORCE A FISH IN CLOSE UNTIL IT STOPS FIGHTING. INSTEAD, EASE OFF A BIT OF LINE TO WEAR HIM DOWN AS YOU REEL IN AGAIN.

FLIES
AND FLY TACKLE

Every fly fisherman has his personal favorites in flies — flies that work best for him. Some anglers have extensive selections of patterns and sizes to suit any occasion. Other anglers use only five or six patterns in limited sizes with good results.

Dull-colored and sparse-hackled flies most closely resemble natural flies. Many anglers have an admiration for beautiful and bright-colored flies, so these patterns are made to sell to them. Such flies may look good to the angler but not to the fish! Exceptions may be the various Coachman patterns which are old stand-bys—such flies as Parmachene Belle, Scarlet Ibis, Montreal, Dusty Miller, White Miller, Cut Throat and Silver Doctor.

Steelhead trout and salmon flies, as well as many varieties of streamers and bucktails, are also bright exceptions but generally dull patterns work best, especially in nymph patterns.

HOW TO SELECT A GOOD FLY ROD.....

THIS IS A FAST-ACTION ROD. IT'S THE BEST CHOICE FOR ALL-AROUND FISHING. RUN A LINE THROUGH ROD'S GUIDES AND TIE IT TO A DISTANT OBJECT. HOLDING ROD GRIP AT A RIGHT ANGLE TO THE LINE, SLOWLY BRING ROD BACK TO BEND TIP. IT'S A TRUE TEST FOR ACTION.

WHEN THE BEND EXTENDS TOWARD THE GRIP, AS HERE, USING THE <u>SAME</u> PRESSURE AS EXERTED IN THE TOP ROD, IT'S A WEAK, WHIPPY ROD WITHOUT BACKBONE NEEDED FOR EASY CASTING. YOU WANT A FAST-ACTION ROD WITH MOST OF THE BEND TOWARD THE TIP BUT THE TIP SHOULD NOT BE TOO LIMBER.

AVOID WHIPPY RODS OR THOSE THAT BEND INTO A NEAT CIRCLE. YOU CAN'T CAST WITH A CIRCLE!

TESTING THE ACTION OF A FLY ROD

Holding rod horizontally, whip it from side to side slowly. Then suddenly shorten the tip's arc by making a shorter but faster continuous action. A wiggling action should result. A pivot point Ⓑ (that part of rod which remains in one spot) identifies its action.

The closer Ⓑ is to Ⓐ, the faster the action.

The closer Ⓑ is to Ⓒ, the action is slower.

A fast-action fly rod is the choice of most fly fishermen.

ROD ACTION PIVOT POINT ← Ⓑ

A FLY ROD'S CARE

ALTHOUGH YOU MAY HAVE SEEN IT DONE, <u>NEVER</u> LAY AN ASSEMBLED FLY ROD ACROSS A ROW OF NAILS ON A WALL. IT CAUSES A 'SET' OR BEND IN BAMBOO. GLASS RODS WON'T BE 'SET' BUT FERRULES AND LINE ON BOTH TYPE RODS MAY BE DAMAGED FROM THE RUSTY NAILS.

BAMBOO RODS ACQUIRE A SET FROM STANDING READY IN A CORNER.

IT'S ALWAYS SAFER TO TAKE RODS APART WHEN NOT IN USE.

FEMALE
FERRULE

SWAB

CLEAN ROD-JOINING FERRULES OFTEN. DIP A SWAB OF TWISTED COTTON ON A TOOTHPICK IN LIGHTER FLUID OR GASOLINE TO CLEAN INSIDE AND A TISSUE TO WIPE OUTSIDES. RUB FERRULES IN HAIR TO LUBRICATE.

51

HOW TO ASSEMBLE AND TAKE APART A FLY ROD

ALWAYS ASSEMBLE THE TIP SECTION TO THE MIDDLE SECTION FIRST.

THE GRIP SECTION IS THE LAST TO BE ASSEMBLED. NEVER ATTEMPT TO RE-ALIGN THE LINE GUIDES AFTER JOINING SECTIONS TOGETHER.

ALWAYS TAKE ROD APART WHEN FINISHED FISHING.

TO TAKE APART, REMOVE THE GRIP SECTION FIRST.

IF A FERRULE STICKS TIGHT, HOLD THE ROD BEHIND YOUR BENT KNEES AND GRADUALLY EXERT PRESSURE, SPREADING YOUR KNEES FARTHER APART UNTIL THE FERRULES PART.

52

THE RIGHT TACKLE
AIDS BUG CASTING

CHOOSE A BASS-ACTION FLY ROD THAT STRAIGHTENS QUICKLY AFTER BEING FLEXED HORIZONTALLY WITH A SIDE-TO-SIDE ACTION WHILE HOLDING THE GRIP AS MOTIONLESS AS POSSIBLE.

SHORT, LEVEL TIP   HEAVY, BUG-TAPER

LONG, LEVEL, RUNNING LINE

DIAGRAM OF A BASS-BUG TAPERED LINE SHOWS 3-DIMENSIONED LINE WITH HEAVY (SIZE "A" OR "B") PART NEAR FISHING END. A TORPEDO OR SHOOTING TAPER IN SIZE GAF OR GBF IS GOOD ALSO. A LEVEL "C" LINE MAY BE USED BUT AS A LAST CHOICE. AVOID LONG, DOUBLE-TAPERS. A ROD-LENGTH LEADER, TAPERING DOWN TO .014 WORKS BEST.

BALANCE WITH AUTOMATIC REEL.

53

SINGLE ACTION OR AUTOMATIC REELS?

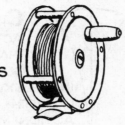

SINGLE ACTION FLY REELS ARE SUPERIOR TO AUTOMATIC REELS WHEN PLAYING LARGE FISH DIRECTLY FROM THE REEL WITH HEAVY TACKLE INSTEAD OF HAND STRIPPING THE LINE. ALTHOUGH IT'S LIGHTER IN WEIGHT, THIS DOESN'T REALLY MAKE MUCH DIFFERENCE.

AUTOMATICS REEL LINE IN AS NEEDED WHEN RETRIEVING IT BY HAND. THEY HAVE BECOME POPULAR WITH MANY VETERAN ANGLERS IN RECENT YEARS. BEGINNERS, BRINGING IN A FISH, FIND THEM LESS TROUBLE.

SEMI-AUTOMATICS MAY BE USED BOTH WAYS FOR ANGLERS LIKING BOTH.

54

CASTING THE LINE TO CAST THE FLY

FLY CASTING LURES ARE SO LIGHT, THE LINE MUST HAVE THE WEIGHT NECESSARY TO CAST THEM SUCCESSFULLY. THEREFORE, CASTING THE LINE CARRIES THE FLY TO ITS MARK.

POWER IN FLY CASTING IS WITHIN THE ROD. TO UTILIZE THIS POWER BEST, A LINE OF SUFFICIENT SIZE OR WEIGHT MUST BE USED TO BRING OUT THE PROPER ROD ACTION.

A NOVICE CAN BECOME GOOD AT FLY CASTING MUCH FASTER WITH WELL-BALANCED EQUIPMENT.'

FISHING LINE TIPS

BRAIDED SILK FLY LINES ARE HEAVIER AND STRONGER THAN NYLON OF THE SAME SIZE. THEREFORE, SMALLER DIAMETER SILK LINE WILL CAST FARTHER BECAUSE IT HAS LESS AIR RESISTANCE THAN NYLON OF THE SAME WEIGHT BUT LARGER SIZE. IT IS ESPECIALLY SUPERIOR ON WINDY DAYS.

SILK FLY LINE MAY BE STRETCHED BETWEEN 2 TREES → FOR DRYING OR APPLYING LINE DRESSING BUT AVOID THIS WITH NYLON OR YOU'LL DAMAGE ITS FINISH!

NYLON REQUIRES NO AFTER CARE WHEN USED IN BRACKISH WATER, OTHER LINES DO.

NYLON IS LESS EXPENSIVE.

56

FLY LINE SIZES AND TESTED STRENGTH

TO THE NEW-COMERS, FLY LINE SIZES INCREASE FROM THE LIGHT OR SMALL DIAMETERED "I" TO THE HEAVIEST OR LARGEST "A" THROUGH SIZES I, H, G, F, E, D, C, B AND A.

SIZE "H" FLY LINE TESTS ABOUT 15 LBS., "G" ABOUT 18 LBS., "F" 24 LBS., "E" 30 LBS., "D" 36 LBS. AND "C" 42 LBS.

WHEN A LARGE FISH BREAKS OFF, IT'S USUALLY THE LIGHT LEADER OR HOOKING FAULT.

57

SELECT A FLY LINE TO MATCH THE ROD

DON'T BE SOLD A VERY LIGHT FLY LINE SUCH AS "I," "H," "G," "F" OR "E" LEVEL LINE FOR A STIFF ACTION ROD. INSTEAD, SELECT A HEAVIER "C" OR "B" LEVEL LINE. A THIN LINE ON A STIFF 9' ROD FEELS LIKE A THREAD ON A CLUB.

ON THE OTHER HAND, A HEAVY FLY LINE IS TOO SLOW ON A VERY LIGHT 8' ROD. HOWEVER, IF YOUR LINE SEEMS TROUBLE- SOME, PERHAPS IT'S TOO LIGHT. IF YOU'RE USING A "D" OR "H-E-H," SWITCH TO A "C" OR "H-C-H" FOR BETTER RESULTS.

58

SHOOTING OR TORPEDO TAPERED LINES

64 ½' OF
F LINE

- - - - - - - -

2½' B TO F
- - - - - -

24'
OF B
LINE
(BELLY)

- - - - - - -

12' OF
TAPER
FROM
G TO
B

- - - - - -

2' OF
B LINE

- - - - - -

LEADER

THE SIZE OF THE LINE IS PURPOSELY EXAGGERATED IN THE SKETCH TO SHOW WHERE THE WEIGHT CENTERS.

THIS PARTICULAR LINE SIZE IS GBF AND IT'S USED ON A MEDIUM ACTION ROD OF 9 FT. OR MORE, OR, A STIFF ACTION ROD OF 8½ FT. OR LESS.

ADVANTAGES OF THIS TYPE FLY LINE ARE: MORE DISTANCE AND IT BUCKS THE WIND BETTER!

59

HOW TO CLEAN AND DRESS A FLY LINE...

Use NAPTHA, CARBON TETRACHLORIDE OR KEROSENE TO DAMPEN (NOT SOAK) A SOFT CLOTH. WIPE THE LINE WITH ONE CLOTH AND DRY IT AT ONCE WITH ANOTHER AS YOU GO. DON'T GET THE LINE TOO WET OR YOU WILL DESTROY ITS FINISH. WORK OUTDOORS WITH THE LINE STRETCHED BETWEEN TREES, PREFERABLY.

Rub COMMERCIAL DRESSING ON A SILK LINE WITH FINGERS ONLY (NO PAD). WIPE SURPLUS OFF WITH A SOFT CLOTH. RUB PARAFIN WAX ON NYLON LINE THEN RUB IT DOWN WITH PAPER. NEVER DRESS A DIRTY LINE.

60

HOW TO REPAIR A TACKY FLY LINE....

OIL FINISHED SILK FLY LINES SOMETIMES BECOME STICKY OR TACKY AFTER BE- ING USED FOR A WHILE. YOU MAY EXTEND THEIR USEFUL- NESS FOR A FEW CENTS.

SOAK TACKY LINES IN A CREAMY SOLUTION OF WHIT- ING AND WATER FOR SEVERAL DAYS. AFTER DRYING FOR A DAY, RUB IT WITH A SOFT CLOTH THEN POLISH WITH A CHAMOIS. APPLY DRESSING.

HOW TO REFINISH A FLY LINE

IF THE FINISH IS RUINED BY ACCIDENTLY REMOVING THE OIL IMPREGNATION

IN THE LINE, LEAVING IT LIMP AND WITHOUT BODY, REFINISH IT AS FOLLOWS:

RUB FROM 4 TO 6 COATS OF BOILED LINSEED OIL INTO THE LINE, ALLOW EACH TO DRY COMPLETELY THEN RUB IT DOWN BEFORE APPLYING THE NEXT COAT OF OIL. WHEN THE LAST COAT HAS HARDENED FOR A WEEK OR SO RUB IT DOWN WITH POWDERED PUMICE ON A CHAMOIS. USE A GOOD LINE DRESSING BEFORE FISHING.

SIZES FOR MAKING TAPERED LEADERS

Here are sizes of monofilament nylon to use in equal lengths for tying personal leaders. Some anglers like shorter mid-strands and longer ends so you may want to experiment to suit _your_ needs.

.017	.015	.013
.008	.009	.011

9' FOR DRY FLY OR NYMPHS UNDER AVERAGE CONDITIONS. LENGTHEN TO 12' FOR WARY TROUT IN CLEAREST, QUIET POOLS OR IN A TAIL-WIND TO SETTLE FLY GENTLY. REMOVE .008 TIP TO SHORTEN FOR HEAD-WINDS OR WET-FLY CASTING.

.019	.017	.015
.012	.013	.014

Above is a heavier, 7½' wet-fly or streamer leader.

.021	.019	.017
.014	.015	.016

This 9' leader is for bass-bugs and steelhead fishing.

63

SPINNER & FLY COMBINATION

SPLIT
SHOT

6"

8"

TROUT, BASS AND OTHER GAME FISH FEEDING IN DEEP POOLS OR FAST WATER GO FOR THIS COMBINATION.

USE ENOUGH SPLIT SHOT AND ALLOW TIME AFTER CAST FOR LURE TO SINK.

RETRIEVED WITH SMALL JERKS AND PAUSES, IT IMITATES A FLY CHASING A MINNOW.

VARY FLY OR SPINNER FOR DIFFERENT COMBINATIONS. LARGE SPINNER AND SMALL FLY, OR VICE VERSA. IT PRODUCES!

64

REJUVENATE FLIES AND STREAMERS WITH THESE TIPS

THE FLY SHOWN IS THE POPULAR "HELLGRAMMITE"

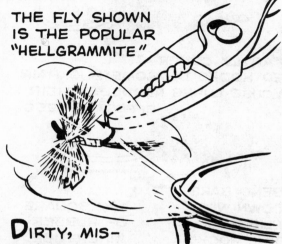

DIRTY, MIS-SHAPENED FLIES OR STREAMERS MAY BE RESTORED BY STEAMING THEM FOR A FEW SECONDS OVER A COVERED PAN OF BOILING WATER OR TEAKETTLE.

ONE DROP OF CLEAR FINGER NAIL POLISH ON A CHIPPED OR LOOSE WINDING PREVENTS IT COMING UNDONE!

65

DOCTORING A LURE

PARTLY COVER-
ED HOOKS ON SOME BUCKHAIR
MOUSE LURES REDUCES THEIR
EFFECTIVENESS.

BEND BARB
DOWN WITH
PLIERS SO
TAIL HOOK'S
EYE AND
RUBBER SQUARE SLIPS OVER IT,
THEN RAISE BARB AGAIN TO KEEP
HOOK FROM SLIPPING OFF.

¼" SQUARE
OF RUBBER
INNERTUBE.

YOU WILL HOOK MORE OF THE
STRIKING FISH BY ADDING A
TANDEM HOOK, POINT TURNED
UP, AS ABOVE. PUNCH A HOLE IN
THE HEAVY-DUTY SQUARE OF
RUBBER TO SLIP IT ONTO THE
LURE'S HOOK. IT KEEPS TAIL
HOOK IN A GOOD POSITION.

TREAT SIMILAR LURES LIKEWISE.

66

FLY-CASTING TIPS

Fly fishing is not as hard to learn as many people believe. First it is necessary to master casting the line with a fly rod. The fly is merely carried by the line to where it gently settles on the water.

Fly fishing will take more fish in heavily-fished waters if the fly is expertly presented. When trout are feeding on nymphs or surface flies it is very difficult to interest them with worms. However, grasshoppers and crickets may work then. This is where fly fishing becomes necessary. The use of wet flies and nymphs is very much like using a worm in technique, and a worm angler can soon learn their use.

When the surface waters are "riffled" to reduce the fishes' vision a short cast will take as many or more fish than a long cast. A child can use a light fly rod with short casts as well as an adult.

Just as important as casting a fly is learning the habits and locations of fish whether they be trout, salmon, or any game fish.

SIDE-TO-SIDE FLY ROD EXERCISE....

THIS EXERCISE SHOULD BE PRAC-
TICED BY BEGINNERS WITH A FLY
ROD SO THEY CAN GET THE FEEL
OF IT. HOLD THE ROD AND SWING
IT BACK AND FORTH BETWEEN
11 AND 1 O'CLOCK IN FRONT OF
THE BODY. KEEP 15 TO 20 FT. OF
LINE IN THE AIR WITHOUT TOUCH-
ING GROUND. YOU SEE THE ACTION
AND FEEL IT AT THE SAME TIME.

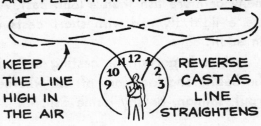

KEEP THE LINE HIGH IN THE AIR

REVERSE CAST AS LINE STRAIGHTENS

FLY CASTING TIPS FOR BEGINNERS....

DON'T TRY FOR DISTANCE UNTIL YOU CAN CONTROL THE SHORTER CASTS. START WITH A SHORT 6 FOOT LEADER AND ABOUT 20 FT. OF LINE. YOU'LL PERFECT YOUR CAST MUCH FASTER AND BE CASTING 50 FT. BEFORE YOU KNOW IT. TOO MUCH LINE IS A BEGINNER'S HANDICAP!

A FLY SHOULD ALWAYS BE USED WHEN PRACTICE CASTING FOR ITS "DRAG" ON THE LINE TO PREVENT IT FROM WHIP-CRACKING OR POPPING ON THE BACKCAST.

FILE HERE

IT'S A GOOD IDEA TO FILE THE BARB OFF THE HOOK'S SHANK BEFORE PRACTICING TO PREVENT ANY INJURIES.

69

STRIPPING IN COILS OF FLY LINE

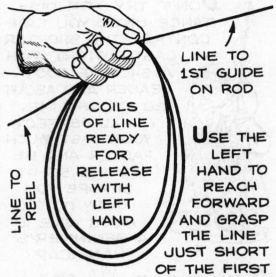

LINE TO 1ST GUIDE ON ROD

COILS OF LINE READY FOR RELEASE WITH LEFT HAND

LINE TO REEL

Use THE LEFT HAND TO REACH FORWARD AND GRASP THE LINE JUST SHORT OF THE FIRST GUIDE. PULL IT BACK TO HOOK IT UNDER ROD HAND'S MIDDLE FINGER. KEEP LEFT-HAND HOLD ON LINE AND, WRAPPING OTHER FINGERS AROUND IT, REACH TO GRASP MORE LINE NEAR THE GUIDE. RELEASE ROD-HAND'S LINE AS YOU PULL NEW LINE BACK TO HOOK UNDER FINGER AGAIN, ETC. CONTINUE MAKING COILS IN RETRIEVING TO BE RELEASED AS NEEDED TO SHOOT OUT IN NEXT FORWARD CAST.

70

THE HAND RETRIEVE FOR FLY FISHING....

GRASP LINE BETWEEN THUMB AND FIRST FINGER. CLOSE 3RD AND 4TH FINGERS FIRMLY ON LINE Ⓐ AND TURN HAND DOWN Ⓑ

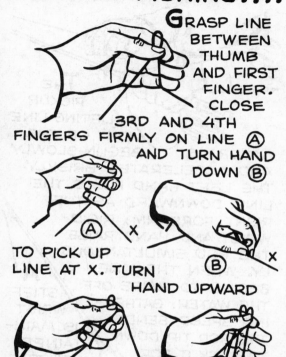

TO PICK UP LINE AT X. TURN HAND UPWARD AS IN Ⓒ. DISCLOSE THE 1ST FOLD AS THE 3RD AND 4TH FINGERS OPEN UP TO GATHER THE NEXT FOLD Ⓓ CLOSING AGAIN AS IN Ⓐ. REPEAT UNTIL LURE IS RETRIEVED, GIVING IT A NATURAL SWIMMING ACTION. RELEASE FOLDS ON NEXT CAST.

71

FLY FISHING: PICKUP FOR THE BACKCAST

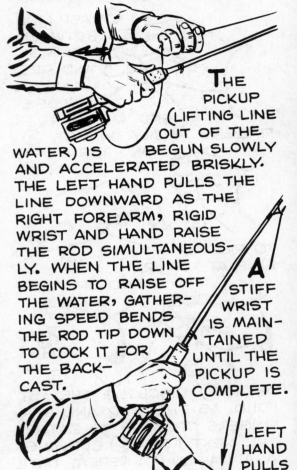

THE PICKUP (LIFTING LINE OUT OF THE WATER) IS BEGUN SLOWLY AND ACCELERATED BRISKLY. THE LEFT HAND PULLS THE LINE DOWNWARD AS THE RIGHT FOREARM, RIGID WRIST AND HAND RAISE THE ROD SIMULTANEOUSLY. WHEN THE LINE BEGINS TO RAISE OFF THE WATER, GATHERING SPEED BENDS THE ROD TIP DOWN TO COCK IT FOR THE BACKCAST.

A STIFF WRIST IS MAINTAINED UNTIL THE PICKUP IS COMPLETE.

LEFT HAND PULLS LINE DOWN

72

FLY CASTING WITH A STIFF WRIST.....

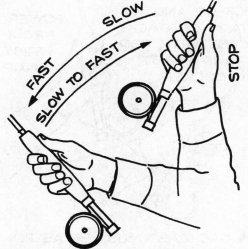
SLOW
FAST
SLOW TO FAST
STOP

KEEP A STIFF WRIST PARAL-
LEL TO THE FOREARM WITHOUT
BENDING IT AND USE THE EN-
TIRE ARM, EXTENDED OR BENT
AT ELBOW, IN CASTING. STOP
BACKCAST WITH ARM VERTICAL
AND ROD ABOUT 20° TO 25° BE-
YOND. IT'S AN IDEAL GENTLE
ACTION FOR CASTING WORMS OR
BAITS THAT SNAP OFF EASILY.
IT'S USED FOR HEAVY SPINNERS
ALSO. AVOID ANY BACK-SNAPS!

START FORWARD CAST AS THE
LINE STRAIGHTENS IN BACK.

73

BACKCAST POWER IN FLY CASTING...

PICK-UP AND START OF BACK-CAST WITH ROD AND WRIST COCKED

POWER FROM WRIST SNAP

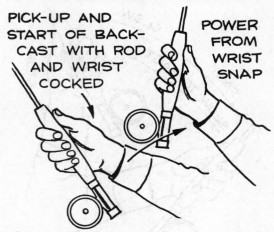

A BACKCAST MUST BE AS POWERFUL AS THE FORWARD CAST. THE GRADUAL INCREASE OF ARC AND POWER IN RAISING A FLY ROD MULTIPLIES WHEN COCKED WRIST SNAPS TO THE VERTICAL STOP POSITION. IT PRODUCES A <u>HIGH</u>–FLYING BACKCAST. DELAY FORWARD CAST UNTIL YOU <u>FEEL</u> THE STRAIGHTENING LINE'S PULL, BENDING THE ROD'S TIP... ... BACK TO COCK IT.

FLY FISHING: A GOOD BACKCAST BEFORE THE FORWARD CAST

FOLLOWING THE PICKUP, THE FOREARM HALTS AS THE GRIP REACHES A VERTICAL POSITION BUT THE ROD'S BACKWARD MOTION IS CONTINUED TO 11 O'CLOCK POSITION BY SNAPPING THE WRIST BACKWARD. THIS ADDED WRIST SNAP SHOOTS THE LINE INTO THE BACKCAST. THIS POSITION IS HELD UNTIL THE LINE TUGS AT THE ROD TIP, THE SIGNAL TO START THE FORWARD CAST.

A WEAK OR LOW (WAITED TOO LONG AFTER THE LINE'S TUG) RESULTS IN A POOR FORWARD CAST.

FLY CASTING TIPS...

IF YOUR FLY OR BUG CONSISTENTLY STRIKES THE GROUND OR WATER ON THE BACKCAST, YOU'RE PAUSING TOO LONG BETWEEN BACKCAST AND FORWARD CAST. PAUSE COINCIDES TO LENGTH OF LINE-- SHORT FOR SHORTER LINE, ETC. THE END PAUSE CUE IS THE LINE'S TUG ON THE ROD. ANOTHER REASON: MAYBE YOU TAKE THE ROD TOO FAR BACK OF THE VERTICAL BEFORE PAUSING.

A PAUSE THAT IS TOO SHORT CAUSES A WHIP-LIKE POPPING.

STUDY YOURSELF IN ACTION.

FLY FISHING: TIMING THE FORWARD CAST

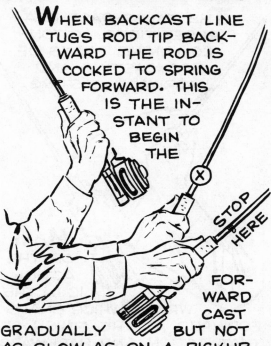

When BACKCAST LINE TUGS ROD TIP BACK-WARD THE ROD IS COCKED TO SPRING FORWARD. THIS IS THE IN-STANT TO BEGIN THE

STOP HERE

FOR-WARD CAST
GRADUALLY BUT NOT AS SLOW AS ON A PICKUP WHEN THE LINE IS INACTIVE. THE FOREARM, COCKED BUT STIFF WRIST AND HAND, ARE MOVED AS ONE IN GATHERING SPEED TO ⊗ WHERE THE WRIST SNAPS ITS POWER IN-TO THE CAST, SHOOTING THE LINE FORWARD. LASTLY, THE PICKUP LINE HELD IN THE LEFT HAND IS RELEASED.

FLY FISHING: USING THE "FALSE" CAST

THE FALSE CAST IS A REPETITIOUS ACTION COMBINING PARTS OF BACKCASTING AND FORWARD CASTING.

MOST OF THE ACTION IS IN THE WRIST WHICH SNAPS FORWARD AT THE FINISH OF THAT ACTION AND BACKWARD AT THE BACK FINISH.

THE LINE STAYS IN THE AIR MOVING BACK AND FORTH OBEYING THE ROD. ITS USES ARE: PAYING LINE OUT AS YOUR LEFT HAND STRIPS IT OFF THE REEL TO CAST FOR-WARD, BUILDING UP SPEED, OR DRYING OF DRY FLIES.

FINDING A HOLE FOR A BACKCAST

MAKING A REVERSE CAST

BRUSH- OR TREE-LINED STREAMS ARE OFTEN DIFFICULT TO FISH BY USUAL CASTING SO THE MOST DIFFICULT SPOTS ARE BY-PASSED BY MANY ANGLERS YET THESE SPOTS MAY HOLD THE BEST FISH!

WHERE THERE IS AN OPENING IN THE TREES, FACE IT WITH YOUR BACK TO THE STREAM. NOW THE BACKCAST IS ACTUALLY THE FOR-WARD CAST. SEEING IT, YOU CAN KEEP IT HIGH AND THROUGH THE OPENING. THEN TURN ABOUT TO SHOOT YOUR FLY ONTO THE WATER.

JUDGING CASTING DISTANCE

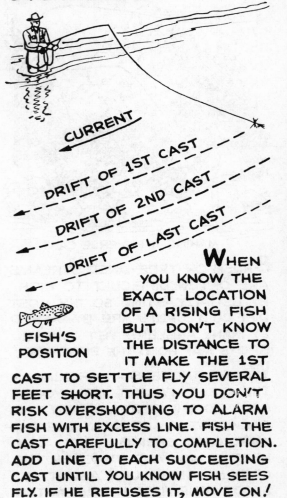

CURRENT

DRIFT OF 1ST CAST

DRIFT OF 2ND CAST

DRIFT OF LAST CAST

FISH'S
POSITION

WHEN YOU KNOW THE EXACT LOCATION OF A RISING FISH BUT DON'T KNOW THE DISTANCE TO IT MAKE THE 1ST CAST TO SETTLE FLY SEVERAL FEET SHORT. THUS YOU DON'T RISK OVERSHOOTING TO ALARM FISH WITH EXCESS LINE. FISH THE CAST CAREFULLY TO COMPLETION. ADD LINE TO EACH SUCCEEDING CAST UNTIL YOU KNOW FISH SEES FLY. IF HE REFUSES IT, MOVE ON!

80

FISH EVERY CAST

IF YOU MAKE A
POOR CAST WITH
FLY OR PLUG
THAT FALLS
WIDE OR
SHORT OF
THE TARGET
DON'T
WHIP IT
HASTILY
BACK TO CAST
AGAIN. TO DO SO
SCARES....

...ALL FISH
IN THE AREA. INSTEAD,
FISH EVERY CAST AS IF IT
IS THE BEST YOU EVER MADE.
THUS, YOU WON'T ALARM THE
INTENDED FISHING AREA AND
YOU MAY UNEXPECTEDLY EN-
TICE ANOTHER FISH TO STRIKE.
THIS ALSO APPLIES TO PICKING
UP A FLY LINE FOR A BACKCAST,
WITHOUT FIRST GUIDING IT SLOW-
LY AWAY FROM THE FISH AREA.

IMPATIENCE RUINS YOUR CHANCES!

FLY-CASTING INTO A HEAD WIND......

BECAUSE MANY DAYS ARE WINDY, A FLY-CASTER MUST COPE WITH IT TO FISH.

HERE IS ONE OF TWO POPULAR SYSTEMS.

RAISE THE ROD TIP HIGH WITH ARM EXTENDED, STOPPING AT VERTICAL ON THE BACKCAST TO KEEP THE LINE HIGH. AS LINE STRAIGHTENS, LOWER AND ARC ROD IN A FORWARD THRUST, ADDING THUMB PRESSURE BEFORE STOPPING THE ROD HORIZONTALLY. GIVE LINE A SHARP LEFT HAND PULL DURING LAST OF THUMB PRESSURE. LINE...

...SHOOTS OUT LOW IN A TIGHT LOOP UNDER THE WIND'S FORCE.

82

FLY-CASTING WITH A BACK WIND......

IN A TAIL WIND, BEGIN THE PICK-UP OF LINE FROM THE WATER BY A SHARP PULL OF THE LINE WITH LEFT HAND AS THE ROD

IS ARCED UPWARD. MORE POWER IS NEEDED IN THE BACKCAST THAN FORWARD CAST SO ROD IS CARRIED FARTHER BACK THAN USUAL AND LINE IS GIVEN ADDED MOMENTUM AS IT SLOWS BY ANOTHER SHARP LEFT HAND PULL. THIS BACKCAST, LOWER THAN USUAL WITH A TIGHT LOOP GETS UNDER THE WIND.

STOP THE FORWARD ARCING ROD HIGHER THAN USUAL. IT SENDS THE LINE HIGH TO RIDE THE WIND AND SETTLE GENTLY.

83

FLY CASTING WITH LEFT SIDE-WINDS

WHEN WIND IS BLOWING FROM YOUR LEFT, TILT YOUR FORE-ARM, WRIST AND ROD TO....

...THE RIGHT AND CAST IN THAT TILTED PLANE, WITH THE BACKCAST AND FORWARD CAST IN THE <u>SAME</u> <u>PATH</u> <u>OF</u> <u>ACTION</u>. DON'T SWING ELBOW IN CASTING, LET IT ACT AS A PIVOT FOR THE FOREARM. YOU MAY TURN SIDE-WISE TO FACE THE CASTING AC-TION IF YOU LIKE.

WIND

IF IT'S A LEFT HEAD-WIND, STOP TILTED BACKCAST AT VERTICAL AND DRIVE THE FORWARD CAST DOWN TO A HORIZONTAL FINISH. WITH LEFT WIND IN BACK, USE

A STRONG LEFT HAND PULL ON...

...THE TILTED BACKCAST.

84

FLY CASTING WITH RIGHT SIDE-WINDS

—WIND→

A BACKHAND CAST IS USED IF A STRONG WIND IS BLOWING FROM YOUR RIGHT. IT'S MADE BY CROSSING THE CASTING ARM IN FRONT OF YOUR BODY TO CAST OVER YOUR LEFT SHOULDER IN MILD WINDS OR PARALLEL WITH THE WATER IN HEAVY WINDS. THE BACKCAST AND FORWARD CAST IS MADE IN THE SAME PATH OF AC-TION WITHOUT CHANGING ANGLE OF ROD'S TILT. SOME ANGLERS PREFER TO USE A CLOCKWISE ROTARY ACTION BY RAISING ROD TILT FOR THE FORWARD CAST.

IN A RIGHT SIDE HEAD-WIND, DRIVE THIS CAST LOWER DOWN AT THE FINISH. IF IT IS A RIGHT SIDE BACK-WIND, USE A LEFT HAND LINE PULL ON BACKCAST.

85

FLY CASTING A RIGHT CURVE CAST

LEADER →

FLY

RISING FISH

A RIGHT CURVE CAST IS AN INCOMPLETED SIDE CAST WITH FLY ROD HELD HORIZONTAL IN EXECUTION. HAND HOLDING SLACK SHOOTING LINE RELEASES IT WHILE A DECIDED CURVE IS STILL IN THE LEADER (BEFORE IT STRAIGHTENS AS IT SHOULD FOR STRAIGHT CASTS). THIS PREMATURE RELEASE KEEPS A CURVE IN LEADER AS FLY DROPS TO THE WATER.

CURRENT

LINE

HERE, THE FLY IS PRESENTED UPSTREAM TO A RISING FISH SO THE LINE IS OUT OF ITS VISION FOR A DRAG-FREE FLOAT.

86

FLY CASTING A LEFT CURVE CAST

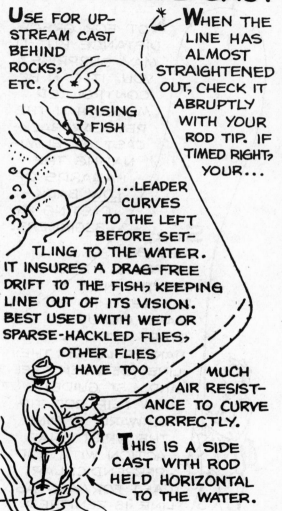

USE FOR UP-
STREAM CAST
BEHIND
ROCKS,
ETC.

WHEN THE
LINE HAS
ALMOST
STRAIGHTENED
OUT, CHECK IT
ABRUPTLY
WITH YOUR
ROD TIP. IF
TIMED RIGHT,
YOUR...

RISING
FISH

...LEADER
CURVES
TO THE LEFT
BEFORE SET-
TLING TO THE WATER.
IT INSURES A DRAG-FREE
DRIFT TO THE FISH, KEEPING
LINE OUT OF ITS VISION.
BEST USED WITH WET OR
SPARSE-HACKLED FLIES,
OTHER FLIES
HAVE TOO
MUCH
AIR RESIST-
ANCE TO CURVE
CORRECTLY.

THIS IS A SIDE
CAST WITH ROD
HELD HORIZONTAL
TO THE WATER.

FLY CASTING: USING THE TOWER CAST

NOT FOR GREAT DISTANCE BUT IT MAY SURPRISE YOU. IT CAN BE CONTROLLED MORE THAN THE REGULAR BACK-CAST BY ELIMI-NATING THE HAZARDS OF <u>LOW</u> BACK-CASTING BY BEGINNERS.

START CAST BY DROPPING ROD TIP AND RAISING GRIP. MAKE PICKUP START WITH A LEFT HAND PULL ON THE LINE (BETWEEN REEL AND 1 <u>ST</u> GUIDE). NOW FLIP ROD TIP SKYWARD, ENDING THE WRIST SNAP ACTION WITH ROD PERPENDICULAR. CAST FORWARD AS LINE IS ZENITHED.

FLY CASTING: USING THE "T" CAST.......

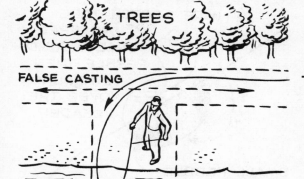

TREES

FALSE CASTING

THE "T" CAST IS USABLE
WHEN HIGH OBSTRUCTIONS PRE-
VENT THE REGULAR BACKCAST.
THE FLY CASTER FACES THE
SHORELINE WITH HIS CASTING
SIDE AWAY FROM THE WATER.
HE BEGINS TO FALSE CAST
WITH HIS ROD AND LINE ACTION
PARALLEL TO THE SHORE
LINE, STRIPPING LINE AND
BUILDING UP SPEED UNTIL HE
IS READY, THEN HE CASTS THE
LINE ACROSS IN FRONT OF HIM-
SELF TO COMPLETE.

USE A PEBBLE TO CAST LIGHT LURES

½" WIDE SCOTCH TAPE WRAPPED ONCE AROUND PEBBLE THEN ½ AROUND OVER THE LEADER.

SMALL PEBBLE

WET LEADER BEFORE FIXING PEBBLE TO IT 5 OR 6 IN. ABOVE A WET FLY OR NYMPH.

BAIT CASTERS CAN SUCCESS-FULLY FISH FLIES AND STREAMERS WITH THIS RIG. EXPERIMENT TO FIND THE BEST SIZE PEBBLES TO USE. TAPE AND PEBBLE SHOULD BE DRY TO HOLD DURING THE CAST. AF-TER ABOUT A MINUTE IN THE WATER, PEBBLE WASHES OFF SO LURE MAY BE FISHED DEEP. GOOD WITH WORMS, ETC. ALSO.

A SINKING LEADER

WHEN FISHING WITH DRY FLIES OR BUGS ON AN UN-RIPPLED SURFACE, FLOATING LEADERS MAY DISTURB THE SURFACE TO WARN THE FISH. IF SO, RUB FISH SLIME, MUD OR SOAP ON THE LAST 2 FT. OF THE LEADER (<u>NOT ON THE LURE</u>) TO MAKE IT SINK QUICKLY. AVOID TREATING TOO MUCH LEADER OR ITS SINKING MAY AFFECT THE FLY'S FLOATING APPEARANCE.

USING STREAMERS OR WET FLIES, THE ENTIRE LEADER MAY BE TREATED TO HELP SINK THE LURE QUICKLY.

FREEING A SNAGGED STREAMER OR FLY

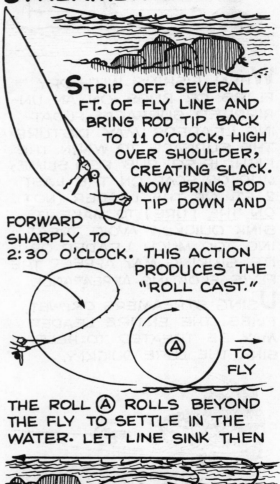

STRIP OFF SEVERAL FT. OF FLY LINE AND BRING ROD TIP BACK TO 11 O'CLOCK, HIGH OVER SHOULDER, CREATING SLACK. NOW BRING ROD TIP DOWN AND FORWARD SHARPLY TO 2:30 O'CLOCK. THIS ACTION PRODUCES THE "ROLL CAST."

TO FLY

THE ROLL Ⓐ ROLLS BEYOND THE FLY TO SETTLE IN THE WATER. LET LINE SINK THEN

A SHARP JERK WILL FREE IT.

PREVENTING "LINE DRAG" ON A DRY FLY

WHEN FISHING DOWNSTREAM, USE A "SNAKE" CAST TO DELAY THE DROP OF THE FLY AFTER THE FORWARD MOVING LINE STRAIGHTENS OUT.

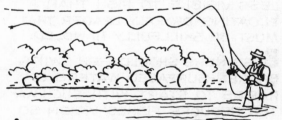

ABRUPTLY STOP THE ROD AND RAISE THE TIP SLIGHTLY TO "SNAKE" THE LINE BEFORE IT DROPS TO FLOAT THE FLY....

— (TOP VIEW) —

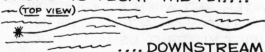

.... DOWNSTREAM FREE OF ANY RESTRAINT OR LINE DRAG CAUSING AN UN- NATURAL "V" FROM ITS FLOAT.

WET FLIES IDEAL
FOR BEGINNERS...

A SUNKEN WET–FLY LEADER IS LESS VISIBLE TO FISH THAN A FLOATING DRY–FLY LEADER THAT MUST BE SKILLFULLY HANDLED.

BEGINNERS SHOULD FISH SWIFT, BROKEN-SURFACED WATERS OR RAPIDS TO START WITH. SUCH WATER REDUCES FISHES' VISION SO YOU MAY MOVE IN CLOSE FOR AN EASY, SHORT CAST WITHOUT ALARMING THEM. FISH HAVE LESS TIME TO STUDY A PASSING FLY IN FAST WATER AND WHEN A FISH STRIKES A WET FLY ON A TAUT LINE IN SWIFT WATER IT USUALLY HOOKS ITSELF WITHOUT ANGLER'S HELP.

THUS, LESS-SKILLED BEGINNERS CAN CATCH FISH WITH WET FLIES.

WET FLY TIPS
FOR BEGINNERS...

FALSE CASTING (WHIPPING A FLY
LINE BACK AND FORTH WITHOUT
THE FLY TOUCHING WATER) DRIES
A FLY QUICKLY. DRY-FLY ANGLERS
USE IT TO KEEP A FLY BUOYANT.
IT MUST BE AVOIDED WITH WET
FLIES SO THE FLY REMAINS WET
TO SINK AS RAPIDLY AS POSSIBLE.
DON'T USE FLY-FLOATING PREPARA-
TIONS ON WET FLIES FOR THE
SAME REASON.

A FAST-MOVING WET FLY USUAL-
LY MEANS A MINNOW TO FISH. A
SLOW-DRIFTING WET FLY MORE
CLOSELY RESEMBLES AN INSECT.
IN FISHING FLIES, REMEMBER, IN-
SECTS FILL ABOUT 90% OF MOST
GAME FISHES' DIET.

WET FLY TRICK!

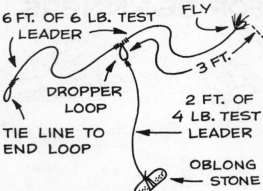

6 FT. OF 6 LB. TEST LEADER

FLY

DROPPER LOOP

3 FT.

TIE LINE TO END LOOP

2 FT. OF 4 LB. TEST LEADER

OBLONG STONE

THIS RIG CAN BE CAST WITH A BAIT CASTING ROD OR SPINNING OUTFIT TO HARD-TO-REACH SPOTS ACROSS A STREAM.

IN USE, IT IS CAST SEVERAL FEET UPSTREAM FROM FEEDING FISH. ITS SPLASH CAUSES FISH TO QUIT FEEDING FOR A TIME. PULL LINE TAUT UNTIL STONE CATCHES BEHIND A ROCK. WAIT UNTIL FEEDING RESUMES. THEN JERK THE LINE TO BREAK THE LIGHT TEST LEADER TIED AROUND THE STONE. THE FLY OR NYMPH (STILL ATTACHED) DRIFTS FREE TO THE FISH. DRY FLIES THAT RESIST PROLONGED SUBMERSION WORK ALSO.

96

RISING A NYMPH

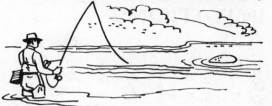

ONE OF THE SIMPLEST BUT IMPORTANT TRICKS IN NYMPH FISHING IS CAUSING THE NYMPH TO RISE FROM THE BOTTOM TO THE SURFACE AS IF TO HATCH.

DETERMINE THE LENGTH OF LINE NEEDED TO REACH THE TAIL OF A RAPIDS OR ROCK LOCATION OF A FEEDING FISH, THEN CAST SO THE NYMPH DRIFTS DEEP AND DRAG-FREE TO IT. KEEP ROD TIP HIGH IN THE LINE'S DIRECTION. AS DRIFT ENDS AND LINE GROWS TAUT, LOWER ROD TIP TO FLOAT LINE AND BEGIN A <u>VERY</u> <u>SLOW</u> HAND RETRIEVE TO IMPART ACTION TO THE RISING NYMPH.

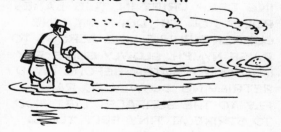

97

FISHING NYMPH IMITATIONS.........

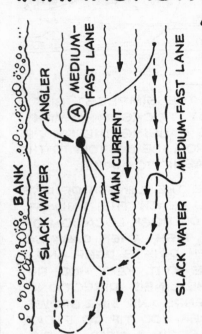

ANGLER WADES QUIETLY TO THE CASTING POSITION TO FISH ACROSS STREAM WITH A SHORT LINE. DURING DOWN-STREAM DRIFT ROD Ⓐ IS HELD HIGH TO PREVENT LINE TOUCHING MAIN CURRENT TO FORM A BELLIED DRAG. END-ING DEEP DRIFT IN THIS LANE, POINT ROD TIP DOWN AT LINE. CURRENT PULLS LINE ACROSS TO RAISE NYMPH. SLOWLY GUIDE FLY INTO QUIET WATER BEFORE HAND RETRIEVING SLOWLY TO RAISE FLY TO THE SURFACE. LIFT ROD TO STRIKE AT TINY FELT TUGS.

ENTICING ACTION FOR A DRY FLY.....

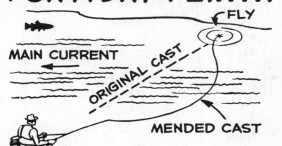

FLY

MAIN CURRENT

ORIGINAL CAST

MENDED CAST

IN FLY-FISHING WIDE STREAMS ACROSS A MAIN CURRENT, MEND THE ORIGINAL CAST AGAINST THE CURRENT TO DELAY ITS DRAG ON YOUR FLY. AS THE DRIFT ENDS, WITHOUT A STRIKE, AND DRAG BEGINS ITS PULL ON FLY, TRY THIS: FEED LINE QUICKLY AND GIVE ROD TIP A SLIGHT UP-JERK EVERY SECOND OR TWO. THIS ADDS VARIETY TO THE DRAG BY PAUSING, DRIFTING AND SKIMMING THE FLY ON THE SURFACE IN AN ENTICING, LIFE-LIKE ACTION!

CURRENT

"WULFF" PATTERNS PERFORM WELL

99

DRY FLY PICK-UP TIP

← FLY
DRIFT
ENDS.

FLY IS
MOVED
AWAY
FROM THE
FISH, THEN SLOWLY
RETRIEVED OUT OF
ITS VISION BEFORE
PICK-UP BEGINS.
THIS IS LESS LIKE-
LY TO ALARM THE
FISH THAN WHISKING
THE LINE BACK
PAST IT SO THAT IT
MAY STRIKE THE
NEXT OFFER-
ING.

LEADER

LINE

ROD

DON'T ALLOW
FLY TO GO SO
FAR BEYOND FISH
THAT THE HEAVY
LINE COMES
WITHIN ITS
VISION...

... BEFORE
MOVING ROD
TIP OUT
SIDEWISE.
RE-ALIGN ROD & LINE
BEFORE THE PICK-UP.

100

FEELING A STRIKE IN WET FLY FISHING

SOME WOMEN ARE BETTER WET FLY ANGLERS THAN MEN BECAUSE THEY ARE MORE SENSITIVE IN FEELING THE LIGHT TOUCH OF MANY STRIKES!

THE USUAL STRIKE OF A TROUT IS A GENTLE NIP OR TUG. IT MAY FEEL VERY MUCH LIKE A FISH JUST BRUSHING AGAINST THE LINE. YOU MUST <u>INSTANTLY</u> SET THE HOOK WHEN YOU FEEL THIS STRIKE!

IF THE CURRENT KEEPS THE LINE TIGHT OR A FISH IS FEEDING FREELY, THE STRIKE FEELS MORE LIKE A GOOD SOLID BUMP.

A SOFT (NOT <u>STIFF</u>) ROD IS RECOMMENDED FOR WET FLY ANGLERS WHO STRIKE TOO HARD.

101

BE PREPARED TO STRIKE INSTANTLY IN FLY FISHING.....

HOLD
LINE
AGAINST
GRIP WITH ROD
HAND FINGER
WHILE SHUTTLE-
RETRIEVING
LINE WITH
LEFT HAND

THE ABOVE TECHNIQUE SHOULD ALWAYS BE USED IN FLY-FISHING WHEN IT MAY BE NECESSARY TO SET HOOK QUICKLY FOLLOWING A FISH'S STRIKE. KEEP THE ROD'S TIP AS LOW AS POSSIBLE AND POINTED AT THE FISH OR WHERE LINE ENTERS THE WATER. THEN WHEN STRIKE IS FELT, MERELY LIFT ROD TIP. SOME ANGLERS SET THE HOOK WITH A PULL OR SLIGHT JERK OF THE LINE WITH THEIR LEFT HAND IN THE ABOVE RETRIEVE. DON'T FISH OR STRIKE SIDEWISE AND YOU WILL HOOK MORE FISH!

102

USING THE REEL TO PLAY BIG FISH ON A FLY ROD!

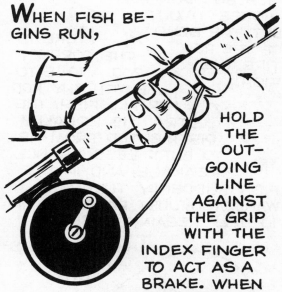

WHEN FISH BE-
GINS RUN,

HOLD THE OUT-GOING LINE AGAINST THE GRIP WITH THE INDEX FINGER TO ACT AS A BRAKE. WHEN THE RUSH ENDS, BEGIN REEL-ING IN THE SLACK TO KEEP PRESSURE ON THE FISH IN-STEAD OF STRIPPING IT IN BY HAND AS WITH SMALLER FISH. WHEN FISH WANTS TO GO, LET OUT LINE AS BEFORE, FROM THE REEL, THEN RETRIEVE WITH THE REEL. THIS IS USED FOR STEELHEADS, SALMON, LARGE BASS AND TROUT.

103

USING ROD PRESSURE

KEEP A CONSTANT PRESSURE AGAINST THE PULLING FISH BUT DON'T "HORSE" IT OUT. LET THE BEND OF THE ROD TIRE THE FISH.

HERE IS THE CORRECT ROD ANGLE TO USE WITH ANY ROD FOR ALL FISH. THE STRAIN IS EQUALLY DISTRIBUTED FROM TIP TO BUTT. LESS CHANCE BREAKAGE, AND IF THE FISH SUDDENLY TURNS TO- WARD YOU, JUST RAISE THE TIP TO HELP REGAIN THE SLACK.

THIS ONE LOOKS PRETTY BUT...

...IT MAY BREAK THE ROD, OR IF THE FISH TURNS QUICKLY, YOU MAY HAVE MORE SLACK THAN YOU CAN HAN- DLE AND LOSE THE PRIZE.

104

A SPINNING ROD'S TEST FOR ACTION

NAIL
SLIDING RINGS

ANY VERTICAL LINE

TIE LINE TO 1ST GUIDE RING

THIS FRENCH TEST IS ACCURATE AND SIMPLE. DRIVE 2 LARGE NAILS INTO A BARN OR GARAGE WALL TO REST ROD HORIZONTALLY BY ITS GRIP (AS SHOWN, TOP). HAVE A PAL HOLD GRIP BETWEEN NAILS DURING TEST TO KEEP IT PLACED. TIE A SPRING SCALE TO LINE, PULLING ROD DOWN UNTIL TIP END IS PARALLEL TO A VERTICAL LINE, THEN READ THE SCALE. 1 OZ. = 28.35 GRAMS. 1 LB. = 453.6 GR. EACH 100 GR. = ABOUT 1 OZ. PER ROD. THUS, A 400 GR. PULL IS A 4 OZ. ROD, ETC.

A 200 ROD IS FOR LIGHTEST LURES. 400 TO 500, MEDIUM. 700 TO 800 IS A SALMON ROD.

105

LOCATION OF THE SPINNING REEL...

YOU USUALLY GET THE BEST ROD ACTION WHEN USING LIGHTEST LURES BY CLAMPING REEL ABOUT 1/3 TO 1/2 UP ON THE GRIP FROM THE BOTTOM.

CLAMP REEL ABOVE THE MIDDLE OF THE GRIP FOR CASTING HEAVIER LURES FOR THE SAME REASON. SOME RODS ARE MADE WITH A GRIP 16" LONG. THESE MAY SUIT YOU BEST IF YOU PLAN TO USE HEAVY SPINNING LURES. SOME ANGLERS PREFER THE LONGER GRIPS FOR 2-HANDED CASTING. AVOID SNAPPING OFF HEAVY LURES BY SLOW BACK-SWINGS.

106

HOW TO PUT LINE
ON SPINNING REELS

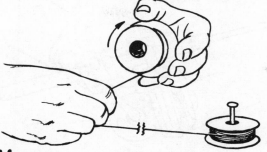

HERE IS HOW TO TRANSFER SPIN-
NING LINE ONTO SPINNING REEL'S
SPOOL WITHOUT CREATING KINKS.
TIE A SLIP NOOSE AROUND SPOOL'S
RECESS AND, KEEPING AN EVEN
TENSION, WIND THE LINE <u>CLOCK-
WISE</u> FOR 20 TURNS, HOLDING THE
REEL SPOOL'S <u>BACK</u> FLANGE. THEN
TURN SPOOL ABOUT AND HOLD BY
ITS FRONT FLANGE. NOW WIND
THE LINE <u>COUNTERCLOCKWISE</u> FOR
20 TURNS. REPEAT THIS ALTERNA-
TING UNTIL REEL SPOOL IS FILLED.

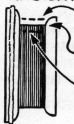

OVERFILLED SPOOL
CAUSES LINE SNARLS.
FILL SPOOL TO ITS LIP
FOR BEST RESULTS.
INSUFFICIENT FILLING
SHORTENS THE CASTS.

USING A BRAKE
WHEN SPIN FISHING

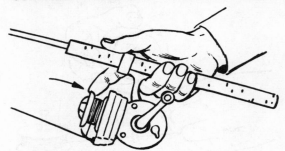

WHEN PLAYING A FISH WITH THE
ANTIREVERSE LOCK SET ON SPIN-
NING REELS, THE PICK-UP DOES
NOT REVOLVE. THE SPOOL TURNS
BACKWARD AS FISH TAKES LINE
AGAINST THE DRAG SETTING. IF
MORE BRAKING IS DESIRED TO
TIRE A POWERFUL FISH BEFORE
HE TAKES ALL YOUR LINE, JUST
EXTEND YOUR FOREFINGER AND
APPLY AS MUCH PRESSURE TO
THE REEL SPOOL AS YOU DARE.
IT IS THE SAME ACTION USED TO
STOP THE LURE'S FLIGHT IN CAST-
ING. YOU CAN TIGHTEN A REEL'S
BRAKE WHILE PLAYING FISH BY
QUICK TAPS OF THE LEFT INDEX
FINGER TIP TO THIS TYPE REEL.

IF A REEL HANDLE IS TURNED TO
BRAKE WITH IT KINKS THE LINE.

108

SPINNING TACKLE FOR FRESH OR SALT WATER FISHING!

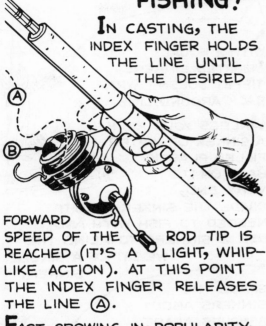

IN CASTING, THE INDEX FINGER HOLDS THE LINE UNTIL THE DESIRED FORWARD SPEED OF THE ROD TIP IS REACHED (IT'S A LIGHT, WHIP-LIKE ACTION). AT THIS POINT THE INDEX FINGER RELEASES THE LINE (A).

FAST GROWING IN POPULARITY, THIS TACKLE FILLS A GAP BE-TWEEN FLY AND BAIT RODS. DUE TO AN ADJUSTABLE DRAG (B), A 4 TO 6 LB. TEST LINE CAN KILL STRIPED BASS, CHANNEL BASS, BARRACUDA, MACKEREL, SNOOK, TARPON AND OTHERS AS WELL AS SALMON OR OTHER FRESH WATER FISH.

109

USING WEIGHTS IN SPIN CASTING....

WITH 2 EQUAL
WEIGHTED SINKERS,
TIPPET DOESN'T WRAP
BACK AROUND LINE.

UNLESS YOUR RIG HAS
A SINKER OR WATER-
FILLED PLASTIC
BALL ON ITS
VERY END,
DIVIDE THE SINKER WEIGHT
NEEDED TO FISH WITH AND
USE 2 SINKERS TOTALING THE
WEIGHT OF A SINGLE
SINKER.

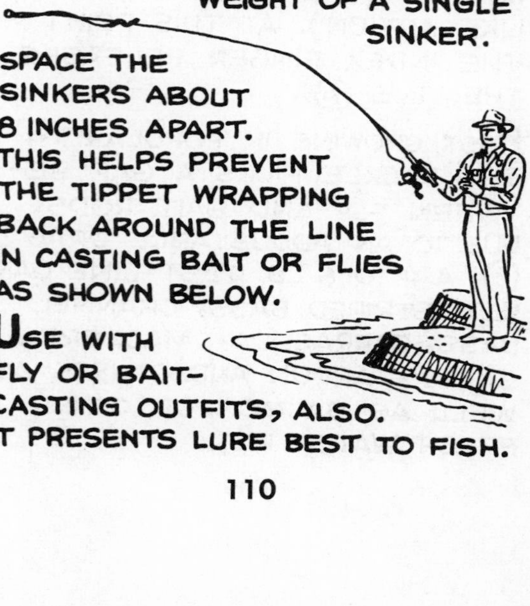

SPACE THE
SINKERS ABOUT
8 INCHES APART.
THIS HELPS PREVENT
THE TIPPET WRAPPING
BACK AROUND THE LINE
IN CASTING BAIT OR FLIES
AS SHOWN BELOW.

USE WITH
FLY OR BAIT-
CASTING OUTFITS, ALSO.
IT PRESENTS LURE BEST TO FISH.

110

POPULAR SPINNING TACKLE LURES....

THE DEVON MINNOW IS ONE OF THE DEADLIEST  REMOVE LURES FOR SPINNING ANGLERS TO USE FOR MOST GAME FISH. IT SHOULD HAVE ALL BUT THE TAIL HOOKS REMOVED. IT WILL SNAG LESS WITH 1 HOOK AND ILLEGAL UNDERSIZED FISH ARE INJURED LESS WHEN RELEASED.

OTHER DEVON MINNOW TYPES, INSPIRED  BY THE ORIGINAL, ARE EQUALLY GOOD. MOST OF THEM CAUSE LINE TO KINK FROM THEIR SPINNING ACTION, THEREFORE BUY OPPOSITE PAIRS AND ALTERNATE THEIR USE TO PREVENT KINKS.

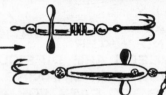 SOME MODELS ARE CLAIMED NON-KINKING; ON OTHERS,  THE SPIN MAY BE REVERSED.

111

THE LIMITATIONS OF SPIN FISHING...

LILY PADS AND WATER WEEDS ARE DIFFICULT TO FISH WITH SPINNING TACKLE. IT'S TOO EASY FOR A HOOKED FISH TO CIRCLE A FEW STEMS AND BREAK THE FINE LINE TO ESCAPE. YOU WILL LOSE SNAGGED LURES, ALSO.

SPINNING TACKLE IS BEST USED IN STREAMS, LARGE RIVERS AND LAKES WITH <u>MINIMUM</u> <u>UNDER-WATER OBSTRUCTIONS</u>. TREELESS BOTTOMS OF <u>MAN-MADE</u> RESERVOIRS ARE GOOD, AS ARE QUARRIES. ALL SNAG-INFESTED WATERS WILL PROVE HAZARDOUS.

112

A SPINNING REEL FOR FLY CASTING

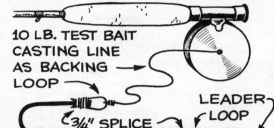

10 LB. TEST BAIT
CASTING LINE
AS BACKING →
LOOP

LEADER
LOOP

¾" SPLICE

25' OF SIZE "B" FLY LINE
FOR 8½ TO 9 FT. RODS UNDER
6 OZ. OR SIZE "A" LINE FOR
RODS OVER 6 OZ. USE BAIT CAST-
ING LINE FOR LOOPS. VARNISH
AND DRY SPLICES 3 TIMES.

WITH REEL SET FOR CAST, HOLD
BACKING LINE AGAINST THE GRIP
WITH INDEX FINGER WHILE
FALSE CASTING ALL THE
FLY LINE JUST BE-
YOND ROD'S TIP.
RELEASE FINGER-
HELD LINE...   ...AT
                        THE PROP-
                    ER MOMENT.
                 IT IS PULLED
              OUT BY THE FOR-
           WARD SHOOTING
         HEAVY FLY LINE FOR
          A LONG CAST.

113

FLY-CASTING WITH A SPINNING ROD...

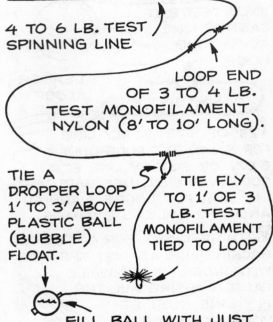

4 TO 6 LB. TEST SPINNING LINE

LOOP END OF 3 TO 4 LB. TEST MONOFILAMENT NYLON (8' TO 10' LONG).

TIE A DROPPER LOOP 1' TO 3' ABOVE PLASTIC BALL (BUBBLE) FLOAT.

TIE FLY TO 1' OF 3 LB. TEST MONOFILAMENT TIED TO LOOP

FILL BALL WITH JUST ENOUGH WATER TO CAST IT.

WHEN CAST, THE BALL LEADS THE FLY (DRY OR WET). AIM CAST TO SETTLE UPSTREAM SO SPLASH WON'T ALARM THE FISH BEFORE DRIFTING DOWN TO THEM.

WORKS WITH CASTING ROD, ALSO!

114

SPIN FISHING THE SMALL POOLS.....

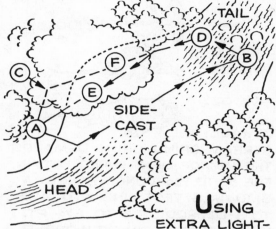

Using EXTRA LIGHT-WEIGHT SPINNING TACKLE YOU CAN FISH SMALL POOLS WITH OVERHANGING BRUSH AS ABOVE. LOCATE YOURSELF Ⓐ ON BANK UPSTREAM NEAR HEAD OF POOL. HANG LURE ABOUT 1-FT. FROM ROD-TIP AND MAKE A SIDE-CAST TO FLIP IT TO THE FAR SIDE OF THE POOL'S TAIL Ⓑ WHERE CURRENT GAINS TO AID LURE FROM SINKING AS YOU TAKE UP SLACK WHEN IT ALIGHTS. HOLD ROD ASIDE Ⓒ TO SWING LURE OVER TO RETRIEVE POSITION Ⓓ. THEN RETRIEVE Ⓔ PAST FISH Ⓕ UNDER OVERHANGING BRUSH.

115

SPIN FISHING THE SMALL STREAMS

1/16 OZ.

1/18 OZ.

1/8 OZ.

Small STREAM SPIN FISHING DEMANDS THE USE OF LIGHT LURES WITHIN THE 1/8-TO 1/20-OUNCE RANGE. A 3-TO 4-LB. TEST LINE WITH A 2- TO 3-OZ. ROD OF 5-TO 6½-FT. LURES MUST SPIN OR WOBBLE EASILY AND RESIST CURRENT ON A TAUT LINE TO AVOID SINKING QUICKLY. IT TAKES A SOFT-ACTION ROD TO BEND IN CASTING THESE LIGHTEST SPINNING LURES.

Always CAST DOWNSTREAM IN- TO THE CURRENT OR FASTER TAIL-WATERS OF SLOW POOLS. LAY FINGER ON SPOOL TO STOP CAST. RAISE ROD TIP AND BEGIN REEL- ING TO ELIMINATE SLACK AND SINK- ING. THEN LOWER TIP, RETRIEVING UPSTREAM THROUGH DESIRED AREA.

116

SPIN CASTING ON SMALL STREAMS

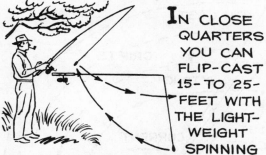

IN CLOSE QUARTERS YOU CAN FLIP-CAST 15- TO 25- FEET WITH THE LIGHT- WEIGHT SPINNING ROD AND LURES. WITH A LURE SWINGING 3- OR 4-FT. BELOW EX- TENDED HORIZONTAL ROD, BRING ROD BACK AND UP THEN THRUST FORWARD, DOWN TO HORIZONTAL. RELEASE LINE AS LURE SWINGS FORWARD TO FLIP IT OUT.

A LIGHTWEIGHT HOLLOW GLASS ROD CAN BE USED TO MAKE A BOW-AND-ARROW CAST UNDER LOW BRANCHES. AVOID EXCESS- IVE ROD BEND THOUGH!

117

SPIN-FISHING THE LARGE STREAMS

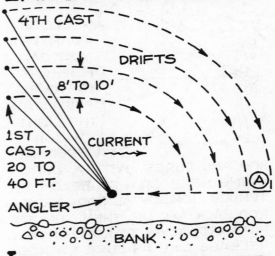

4TH CAST

DRIFTS

8' TO 10'

1ST CAST, 20 TO 40 FT.

CURRENT

ANGLER

Ⓐ

BANK

IF STREAM IS FAST AND DEEP, CAST FARTHER UPSTREAM SO LURE CAN SINK DEEP WHERE FISH LIE BEHIND ROCKS ON THE BOTTOM. IN DEEP RIVERS, FEED SEVERAL EXTRA FEET OF SLACK LINE OUT AFTER CAST BEFORE CLOSING REEL'S PICK-UP FOR A DEEPER DRIFT. BEGIN SLOW RE-TRIEVE DURING DRIFT, AFTER AL-MOST SINKING TO THE BOTTOM. START RETRIEVING AT ONCE IN SHALLOW, SNAG-STREAMS. LET LURE SWIM AFTER EACH DRIFT. MAKE NEXT CASTS FROM Ⓐ.

118

TROLLING TIP...HOW TO REDUCE SPEED WITHOUT STALLING

Chapter 7

Trolling,
Ice Fishing,
and Other
Fishing
Methods

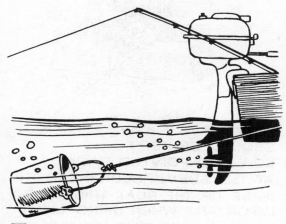

TIE A BUCKET ON A LENGTH OF ROPE AND LET IT DRAG BEHIND THE BOAT. ADJUST THE ROPE SO IT CANNOT FOUL THE PROPELLER.

SOMETIMES IT'S NECESSARY TO TROLL <u>VERY</u> SLOW WHEN FISHING FOR CRAPPIES, WALL-EYES AND YELLOW PERCH. OTHER FISH SUCH AS BASS, LARGE TROUT, ETC., MAY PRE-FER A SLOW MOVING LURE AT TIMES SO IF A MOTOR STALLS AT SLOW SPEED, TRY THIS.

TROLLING TIPS....

Chapter 7

Trolling,
Ice Fishing,
and Other
Fishing
Methods

ROD TIP
SHOULD BE KEPT
LOW AND POINTED BACK
AT THE SUBMERGED LINE IN THE
WAKE OF THE BOAT. THIS IS VERY
IMPORTANT WHEN USING LIGHT
BAMBOO RODS THAT MIGHT "SET"
IN A PERMANENT BEND OTHER-
WISE FROM CONSTANT BENDING.

TROLLING THUS, JUST A SLIGHT
LIFT OF THE ROD WILL SET THE
HOOK QUICKLY IN THE MOUTH OF
A STRIKING FISH BECAUSE THERE
IS NO SLACK IN A BENT ROD TO
SOFTEN YOUR STRIKE. THE ROD'S
HEAVIER BUTT SECTION TAKES
THE JAR OF A STRIKE TO RE-
DUCE ROD-TIP BREAKAGE.

SIT FACING PADDLER IN A CANOE,
TROLLING OPPOSITE PADDLING SIDE.

LEARN HOW DEEP YOU'RE TROLLING

Chapter 7

Trolling,
Ice Fishing,
and Other
Fishing
Methods

MOST TROLLING ANGLERS OVERESTIMATE THE DEPTH THEY THINK THEY ARE FISHING BECAUSE THEY MAY HAVE SEVERAL HUNDRED FEET OF LINE OUT.

YOU CAN FIND EXACTLY HOW DEEP YOUR LURE IS MOVING BY GRADUALLY TROLLING CLOSER TO SHORE. WHEN YOUR LURE BECOMES SNAGGED ON THE BOTTOM, MOVE BACK UNTIL YOU'RE RIGHT ABOVE IT. MAKE A SURFACE MARK ON THE LINE THEN WHEN YOUR LURE IS FREE MEASURE THE LINE UP TO THE MARK.

121

TROLLING TRICKS

Chapter 7

Trolling,
Ice Fishing,
and Other
Fishing
Methods

MARK YOUR LINE BY TYING A BIT OF CONTRASTINGLY COLORED SILK THREAD AROUND IT. PLACE ONE WRAPPING AT 50 FT., TWO AT 75 FT., THREE AT 100 FT. ETC. WHEN TROLLING VERY DEEP, START MARKING AT 100 FT. COVER WRAPS WITH 2 COATS OF SHELLAC TO AVOID SLIPPAGE AND INSURE SMOOTH PASSAGE IN GUIDES.

AFTER BOATING A FISH, IT'S EASY TO RETURN THE <u>SAME</u> AMOUNT OF LINE TO THE FISHES' FEEDING DEPTH WHICH MAY VARY FROM DAY TO DAY.

OFFSET HOOKS Ⓐ TEND TO TWIST A LINE MORE THAN STRAIGHT HOOKS.

122

TROLLING TRICKS

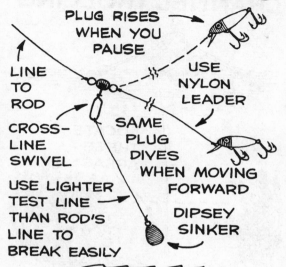

PLUG RISES WHEN YOU PAUSE

LINE TO ROD

CROSS-LINE SWIVEL

USE NYLON LEADER

SAME PLUG DIVES WHEN MOVING FORWARD

USE LIGHTER TEST LINE THAN ROD'S LINE TO BREAK EASILY

DIPSEY SINKER

Adjust leader and sinker line's length so plug runs just above bottom hazards. When fish are deep you will know your plug is where it should be when sinker drags bottom occasionally. When it snags, break sinker line to save plug.

Troll float-and-dive midget plugs slowly with frequent pauses.

Trolled spinning lures don't twist line with this rig!

123

CHANNEL TROLLING

Chapter 7

Trolling,
Ice Fishing,
and Other
Fishing
Methods

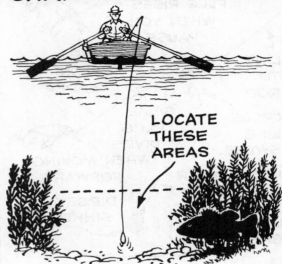

LOCATE
THESE
AREAS

WEED BORDERED CHANNELS IN
RIVERS AND LAKES ARE BEST COV-
ERED IN FISHING BY TROLLING.
THIS AREA MAY BE NARROW AND
20 FEET OR MORE DEEP. PLUG
CASTING FROM SHORE USUALLY IS
INEFFECTIVE (EXCEPT WHEN FISH
ARE MOVING ABOUT ON A FEEDING
SPREE) BECAUSE PLUG CROSSES
ABOVE CHANNEL FOR ONLY A
SHORT DISTANCE. FISH, HIDING IN
WEED BORDERS USUALLY AREN'T
INTERESTED, EVEN IF IT'S SEEN!
A LURE TROLLED DEEP WITHIN A
CHANNEL IS MORE PRODUCTIVE!

124

ICE FISHING TOOLS—THE CHISEL AND STRAINER

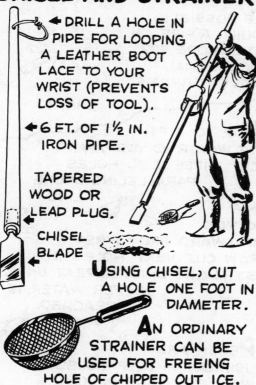

← DRILL A HOLE IN PIPE FOR LOOPING A LEATHER BOOT LACE TO YOUR WRIST (PREVENTS LOSS OF TOOL).

← 6 FT. OF 1½ IN. IRON PIPE.

TAPERED WOOD OR LEAD PLUG. →

CHISEL BLADE →

USING CHISEL, CUT A HOLE ONE FOOT IN DIAMETER.

AN ORDINARY STRAINER CAN BE USED FOR FREEING HOLE OF CHIPPED OUT ICE.

SAFETY FIRSTS: LESS THAN THREE INCHES OF ICE IS UNSAFE. EVEN THIS MAY BE RISKY OVER MOVING CURRENTS. BE WARY OF INLET OR SHORELINE ICE, PLAY IT SAFE, AVOID ANY UN-NECESSARY CHANCES.

Chapter 7

Trolling,
Ice Fishing,
and Other
Fishing
Methods

LOCATING HOLES FOR ICE FISHING

IF POSSIBLE, BUILD A FIRE ON THE SHORE FOR OCCASIONAL BODY WARMINGS.

SHORE

IN 2 TO 3 FT. OF WATER 10 YDS. APART, CUT THREE 12 IN. HOLES PARALLELING SHORE LINE.

10 YDS. OUTWARD FROM FIRST ROW CUT NEXT HOLES IN STRAIGHT LINE. REPEAT UNTIL DEEPER WATER IS REACHED.

PERCH ARE USUALLY IN DEEP HOLES. WALLEYES AND PICKEREL MAY FEED IN SHALLOW WATER. INSPECT BAIT AT REGULAR INTERVALS.

REMOVE DEAD MINNOWS OR WORMS FOR BEST RESULTS.

126

AN INTRODUCTION INTO ICE FISHING TECHNIQUE

A TIP-UP IN "READY" POSITION

Chapter 7

Trolling,
Ice Fishing,
and Other
Fishing
Methods

IF MORE THAN ONE TIP-UP OR "TRAP" IS TO BE USED, CHECK HOLE FREQUENTLY TO REMOVE NEW ICE FORMINGS.

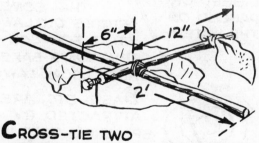

6" 12" 2'

CROSS-TIE TWO SAPLING PIECES AS ABOVE. THIS IS NOT AS GOOD AS A COMMERCIAL SPOOL TYPE HOLDING 30 FT. OF 18 LB. TEST LINE PERMITTING A SHORT RUN, BUT IT WILL CATCH SMALL FISH. BAIT WITH WORM OR MINNOW. TRY VARIOUS DEPTHS. CHECK YOUR STATE LAWS ON ICE FISHING.

127

JIGGER FISHING WITH A CANE POLE

Chapter 7

Trolling,
Ice Fishing,
and Other
Fishing
Methods

ANGLER SITS IN A SLOW MOVING BOAT'S BOW HOLD-ING A <u>LONG</u> CANE POLE OUT IN FRONT. A FEATHER-ED TREBLE HOOK IS JIGGED OR DANCED ON THE WATER.

IT'S SO EFFECTIVE THAT SOME STATES OUTLAW-ED IT FOR CON-SERVATION'S SAKE. (CHECK LOCAL LAW!)

BASS, ETC. ARE ATTRACTED BY SPLASHING POLE IN WATER OCCASION-ALLY.

16 IN.

128

A "SKITTERING" RIG

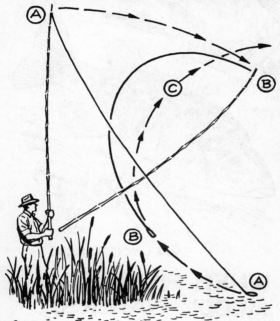

Chapter 7

Trolling,
Ice Fishing,
and Other
Fishing
Methods

A 15 TO 20 FT. CANE POLE AND A
LINE A FEW FEET LONGER ARE USED
TO THROW THE BAIT, SPINNER OR
SPOON FORWARD TO THE WATER
WITH A "ROLL" CAST AS SHOWN.
CAST IS MADE BY RAISING ROD TIP
TO Ⓐ AND SWEEPING FORWARD
Ⓑ TO FLIP THE LURE IN AN ARC
FROM Ⓐ BEYOND Ⓒ TO DESIRED
AREA. LURE IS "SKITTERED" IN RE-
TRIEVE ON THE SURFACE OR IT
MAY BE SWEPT FROM SIDE TO SIDE.

Chapter 7

Trolling,
Ice Fishing,
and Other
Fishing
Methods

SMALL MOUTH BASS

WHEN FISHING IN MUDDY WATERS...

....BEST RESULTS MAY BE FOUND UNDER OVERHANGING BANKS, AROUND SUBMERGED STUMPS OR TREES AND LARGE BOULDERS. WATER IS USUALLY MOST CLEAR IN THESE SPOTS, AND THIS IS WHERE FEEDING FISH CAN SEE YOUR LURE.

USUALLY, FISH DON'T MOVE ABOUT MUCH AT THIS TIME SO IT IS WISE TO KNOW WHERE THEY MAY BE.

MUDDY STREAM FISHING TIPS . . . . .

Chapter 7

Trolling,
Ice Fishing,
and Other
Fishing
Methods

MUDDY STREAMS OF SPRING RUN-OFFS ARE BEST FISHED WITH WET FLIES AND BAIT. LARGE BRIGHT-COLORED FLIES ARE EASILY SEEN IN THE MURKY WATER. LEADERS SHOULD BE USED EVEN THOUGH THEY ARE LESS VISIBLE. USE SPLIT SHOT IF NEEDED TO CARRY YOUR FLY, NYMPH OR BAIT NEAR THE BOTTOM WHERE THE CURRENT LESSENS EVEN IN FAST STREAMS. FISH UNDER CUT BANKS WHERE FISH LIE IN WAIT FOR WORMS THAT WASH AWAY WHEN PARTS OF A BANK BREAK OFF.

131

NIGHT FISHING TIPS

Chapter 7

Trolling,
Ice Fishing,
and Other
Fishing
Methods

WHERE NIGHT FISHING IS LE-GAL, IT IS USUALLY THE BEST TIME FOR CATCHING THE LARG-EST OF MOST SPECIES.

YOU SHOULD KNOW A STREAM AND ITS BANKS TO AVOID USING A FLASHLIGHT. LEARN TO TIE ON LURES AND NET FISH IN DARK-NESS. SOME FISH QUIT FEEDING WHEN A LIGHT IS SHOWN. DON'T SMOKE. MOVE ABOUT QUIETLY!

IT'S EASIER TO HANDLE A SHORT FLY LINE IN THE DARK BUT KEEP IT TAUT SO THAT A SILENT STRIKE MAY BE FELT. QUITE OFTEN A FISH WILL BE HOOKED CLOSE BY DUE TO REDUCED VISIBILITY. FLIES SHOULD BE USED IN QUIET POOLS. COLOR AND PATTERN MEAN LESS AT NIGHT. USE NOISY LURES FOR PLUG CASTING!

NIGHT FISHING WITH A LANTERN

Chapter 7

Trolling,
Ice Fishing,
and Other
Fishing
Methods

THIS METHOD IS VERY EFFECTIVE WHERE IT IS LEGAL!

TIE A GASOLINE LANTERN TO A POLE SUSPENDED FROM THE BOAT. USE A REFLECTOR TO KEEP LIGHT AND ITS ATTRACTED BUGS AWAY FROM YOU, ONTO THE WATER. ANCHOR IN A CHOICE LOCATION TO AWAIT ACTION. GAME FISH COME TO FEED UPON FALLEN INSECTS AND ATTRACTED SHAD OR OTHER MINNOWS. USE A FLY ROD WITH FLIES OR BUGS. OR, BAIT WITH A MINNOW. USE A LEADER WITHOUT FLOAT OR SINKERS.

IF GAME FISH DON'T COLLECT, CRUISE VERY SLOWLY SO MINNOWS CAN FOLLOW TO FIND THEM.

FISHING FOR BASS, PIKE, AND OTHER PAN FISH

Large-mouthed bass are found in and around weeds and lily pads of slow-moving streams and rivers, lakes and ponds. Small-mouthed bass prefer cool, faster-moving streams and rivers (often downstream from colder trout waters) with rocks and sandy bottoms, lakes with sand bars and rocky ledges or submerged boulders.

Muskellunge, northern pike and pickerel haunts are weedy waters with logs and snags for hiding places. Here you will probably lose plugs, but snagged lures are worth the risk if you catch more fish. The risk of losing terminal gear is greatly lessened if you follow the old timers' practice of using a heavy-duty line with a leader of a short nylon monofilament of a breaking test a bit lower than the line. Then a snagged lure can usually be pulled free instead of breaking off. If it can't, the leader will break and you will save the line. A wire leader on the monofilament's end is best for "musky," pike, pickerel and walleyes who have sharp teeth that can cut ordinary lines or leaders. Keep your fingers out of those savage mouths, also!

HARASSED BASS

NORMALLY BOLD, BASS BECOME SHY FROM THE CONSTANT DISTURBANCE OF MOTORBOATS, ETC., AROUND MANY RESORTS DURING THE DAY. THEN THE BASS SEEK THE DEPTHS OF QUIETER COVES, REFUSING NOISY SURFACE PLUGS.

FISH THE QUIETEST COVES WITH A BASS BUG ON THE SURFACE OR SMALL, NOISELESS LURES, DEEP WITH SPINNING TACKLE. AS DISTURBANCES QUIT AT NIGHTFALL, BASS BEGIN FEEDING FIRST IN THESE COVES AND ALONG THE WEEDY SHORELINES.

135

BASS FISHING TIPS FOR LAKES

LILY PAD BORDER'S EDGE

RIDGE ENDS

FISH HERE

UNDERWATER WEED-BED

WEEDS END ON STEEP PITCH-OFF

WITH WARMING WATER, LARGE-MOUTH BASS MOVE TO COOLER DEEP WATER NEAR FAVORED WEED BEDS. WEEDS DO NOT GROW WHERE THE DIMINISHED SUN LIGHT CAN'T STIMULATE THEM. ON A STEEP DROP-OFF, WEED GROWTH ENDS ABRUPTLY AT THIS DEPTH. IT VARIES FROM ABOUT 15 TO 20 FEET OR MORE, OCCURRING DEEPEST IN CLEAR-EST LAKES. QUICK DROP-OFFS ARE LOCATED OFFSHORE WHERE A STEEP RIDGE JUTS OUT INTO A LAKE OR WHERE WEEDS RISE FROM SUBMERGED ISLANDS.

136

STILL FISHING WITH BAIT FOR LARGEMOUTH BASS

A BOBBER SHOULD ALWAYS BE USED IN STILL FISHING OVER WEED BEDS. WITHOUT A BOBBER, THE BAIT QUICKLY SINKS INTO THE WEEDS WHERE IT CANNOT BE SEEN TO LURE THE BASS. ADJUST THE BOBBER SO THE BAIT FLOATS JUST CLEAR OF THE WEEDY LARGEMOUTH BASS HAUNTS. LIFT BAIT OCCASIONALLY TO BE SURE IT IS FREE. IT MAY ATTRACT FISH ALSO!

BOBBER

LOST IN THE WEEDS

137

STILL-FISHING A MINNOW FOR BASS

Chapter 8

Fishing for Bass, Pike, and Other Pan Fish

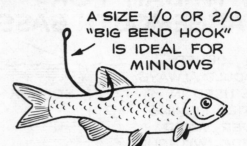

A SIZE 1/0 OR 2/0 "BIG BEND HOOK" IS IDEAL FOR MINNOWS

MANY ANGLERS USE MINNOWS TOO SMALL FOR THE BEST BASS FISHING. USE ONLY 3 TO 4 INCHERS. THEY ATTRACT BEST AND ARE A WORTH-WHILE MOUTHFUL FOR BASS. SMALLER MINNOWS ARE FOR CRAPPIES AND OTHER FISH. HOOK AS SHOWN, JUST UNDER SKIN IN BACK OF DORSAL FIN. USE HOOKS AT LEAST 5/8 IN. ACROSS BEND, ON MONOFILAMENT LEADERS WITH SINKER TO HOLD MINNOW ON BOTTOM OR JUST ABOVE WEEDS. USE QUILL-TYPE FLOAT THAT SUBMERGES AT THE SLIGHTEST PULL. CAST GENTLY TO AVOID MINNOW LOSSES.

SHORE-LINE BASS

WITH THE COOLER WEATHER OF FALL, BASS CRUISE ALONG THE SHORE—

LINES AWAY FROM THEIR SUMMER HAUNTS OF DEEP COOL WATER. FROGS ARE FAVORED PREY OF WAITING BASS DURING THE LATE AFTERNOON AND EVENING.

FROG-LIKE PLUGS, CAST NEAR SHORE AND PERMITTED TO REST A MOMENT BEFORE BE-ING RETRIEVED, ARE GOOD. TRY TO MOVE THE PLUG LIKE A FROG. IF YOU'RE FISHING FROM A BOAT, CAST THE PLUG ON THE SHORE AND JERK IT INTO THE WATER WITH VARIOUS RETRIEVES.

SHORELINE BASS

Chapter 8

Fishing
for Bass,
Pike, and
Other Pan
Fish

AT DAWN AND EVE-
NING, DEEP-WATER BASS OFTEN
FEED AMONG LILY PADS DURING
HOT WEATHER. IN SHALLOW WA-
TERS, BASS MAY REMAIN IN THE
SHADE OF PADS TO FEED IN DAY-
TIME. USE A 6 TO 7½ FT. LEADER,
TESTING 6 OR MORE LBS. TO BUG-
CAST THE EDGES. IT BREAKS LESS
IN PRESSURING HOOKED FISH TO
LEAD HIM INTO OPEN WATER FOR
THE PLAY. OR, A HEAVY-TEST BAIT-
CASTING LINE WITH CASTING RODS
FOR WEEDLESS LURES (POPPING
PLUGS AND SILVER OR BRASS
SPOONS WITH PORK RIND STRIP)
MAY BE USED AMONG PADS.

PUT A FRESH-KILLED FROG ON A
WEEDLESS HOOK. BAIT-CAST IT IN-
TO PADS AND PULL IT UP ON A
PAD A MINUTE OR SO THEN PULL
IT OFF FOR A WAITING BASS.

STREAM SIGNS FOR BASS FISHING

SMALLMOUTH BASS ARE SOME-
TIMES CAUGHT IN TROUT–LIKE
WATER BUT AS A RULE, STREAM
BASS PREFER LESS CURRENT.
BASS AND PANFISH USUALLY
PREFER DEEP DARK POOLS IN
SLOWER-MOVING WATER. UNDER
AN OVER-HANGING TREE WHERE
INSECTS, SMALL BIRDS, WORMS,
ETC. DROP INTO QUIET WATERS
IS A GOOD PLACE TO FISH. ROOTS
MAY BE WASHED OUT TO FORM
A PROTECTIVE COVER FOR FISH
UNDER SOME TREES.

WHERE A TREE HAS TOPPLED,
DEBRIS AND FOOD COLLECTS
AROUND IT. FISH HERE WHERE
A HOLE IS GOUGED UNDERNEATH.

AUTUMN'S SMALL-MOUTH BASS TIPS

Chapter 8

Fishing
for Bass,
Pike, and
Other Pan
Fish

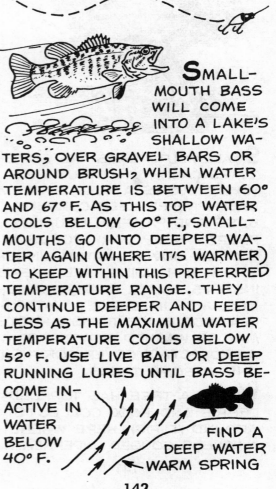

SMALL-MOUTH BASS WILL COME INTO A LAKE'S SHALLOW WATERS, OVER GRAVEL BARS OR AROUND BRUSH, WHEN WATER TEMPERATURE IS BETWEEN 60° AND 67° F. AS THIS TOP WATER COOLS BELOW 60° F., SMALL-MOUTHS GO INTO DEEPER WATER AGAIN (WHERE IT'S WARMER) TO KEEP WITHIN THIS PREFERRED TEMPERATURE RANGE. THEY CONTINUE DEEPER AND FEED LESS AS THE MAXIMUM WATER TEMPERATURE COOLS BELOW 52° F. USE LIVE BAIT OR <u>DEEP</u> RUNNING LURES UNTIL BASS BECOME INACTIVE IN WATER BELOW 40° F.

FIND A DEEP WATER WARM SPRING

142

FISHING PLUGS FOR SMALLMOUTH BASS

GOOD SMALLMOUTH BASS STREAMS, BEING TROUT-LIKE, CALL FOR UNDER-WATER PLUGS. IN SWIFT WATER AND RIFFLES THESE BASS LURK BEHIND SHELTERING ROCKS WAITING FOR BITS OF FOOD TO PASS BY.

A POPULAR PLUG IS A SMALL 3/8 OZ. OR LESS OF THE SINK-ING TYPE SUCH AS THIS ONE.

IN SWIFT DEEP WATER, CAST UP-STREAM, RETRIEVE JUST A BIT FASTER THAN THE FLOW. IN SHALLOWS, CAST DOWNSTREAM.

143

PLUG-CASTING DEEP HOLES FOR BASS...

Chapter 8

Fishing
for Bass,
Pike, and
Other Pan
Fish

QUIETLY ANCHOR BOAT IN SHALLOW WATER WITHIN CASTING DISTANCE OF A DEEP HOLE OR STEEP PITCH-OFF WHERE UNDERWATER WEED GROWTH ENDS ABRUPTLY, THUS AVOIDING PASSING OVER TO ALARM FISH IN ADVANCE.

PAUSE

SLOW RETRIEVE 4- TO 5-FT.

REST

WHEN YOUR CAST LURE (METAL WITH PORK RIND, ETC. PREFERRED) SINKS TO THE BOTTOM, THE LINE GOES SLACK. REST LURE BEFORE SLOWLY RAISING ROD AND REELING IN SLACK IN LOWERING AGAIN TO PAUSE, ETC. QUIETLY AND QUICKLY NET HOOKED FISH TO AVOID ALARMING OTHER FISH IN THE AREA.

144

BASS-BUGGING FROM A BOAT

Chapter 8

Fishing
for Bass,
Pike, and
Other Pan
Fish

IN SUMMER, BASS BUG FISHING IS USUALLY BEST FROM DAWN UNTIL MID-MORNING AND FROM LATE AFTERNOON UNTIL DARK, DURING DAYTIME HOURS. HOT NIGHTS ARE EXCELLENT. CRUISE SLOWLY IN SHALLOW (5' OR LESS) WATER AT SUCH TIMES.

IF THE WATER IS CLEAR AND MIRROR CALM, LONG CASTS OF 65 TO 80 FT. MAY BE NEEDED BECAUSE BASS CAN SEE A BOAT MORE EASILY THEN THAN WHEN THE SURFACE IS RIPPLED. IN A LAKE OF RISING FISH AND NONE NEARBY, THE BOAT HAS SPOOKED THEM SO LENGTHEN YOUR CASTS!

APPROACH ALL AREAS QUIETLY!

145

POPPING BUGS TO GET THE BASS. . . .

A POPPING BUG IS ONE OF THE DEADLIEST LURES WHEN BASS ARE FEEDING ON OR NEAR THE SURFACE. WHEN YOU HEAR OR SEE THE SPLASH OF A RISING BASS, CAST TO IT AS SOON AS YOU CAN. LET BUG LIE MOTIONLESS FOR A COUNT OF 10 THEN 'POP' IT ONCE. POP AGAIN AT 10 AND SO ON. BASS MAY STRIKE BEFORE 1ST POP IF CAST IS QUICK AND ACCURATE. KEEP ROD-TIP LOW FOR STRIKE, POPPING BUG WITH A QUICK JERK OF LINE IN LEFT HAND AS YOU GIVE ROD-TIP A SLIGHT WHIP.

LET BUG LIE STILL FOR 15 OR 20 MINUTES. THIS OFTEN IRRITATES A NON-STRIKING BASS INTO STRIKING IT TO GET IT OUT OF HIS SIGHT!

146

SPINNER & FLY FOR SMALLMOUTH BASS

Use a "YELLOW SALLY," GRAY, BROWN

OR OTHER COLOR (NOT WHITE) HACKLE BASS FLY, SIZE 1/0, TIED WITHOUT WINGS. OTHERWISE, CAREFULLY CLIP OFF THE WINGS SO BINDINGS ARE NOT LOOSENED. HACKLE SHOULD BE 1" ACROSS TO OPEN AND CLOSE IN THE WATER AS YOU CONTINUOUSLY TWITCH IT AN INCH OR SO AND RELEASE IT.

Attach fly to a highly polished silver spinner, size no. 2 for average waters or no. 3 for roily waters. Use double spinners on a shaft in fast streams. SPINNER MUST SPIN FREELY! GREASE LINE TO FLOAT IN STREAMS OR LAKES. USE SPLIT SHOT ON LEADER 18" ABOVE LURE FOR TROLLING.

BASS FISHING TIPS

SMALLMOUTH BASS

DRIFT A SPINNER AND FLY COMBINATION DOWN A RAPIDS INTO A POOL. DIRECT ITS COURSE, KEEPING TENSION ON THE LINE AND GIVING LURE AN ADVANCE AND FALL-BACK ACTION. DRIFT IT ABOUT BOULDERS INTO POCKETS DOWNSTREAM.

LARGEMOUTH BASS

LARGEMOUTHS MAY NOT USUALLY GO FOR THE SPINNER AND FLY BUT TRY CASTING IT TO A LAKE'S <u>EDGE</u> OR NEAR WEEDS FROM A BOAT. USE SHORT RETRIEVE AND PAUSE ACTION. TRY LURES OTHERS NEVER USE!

FISHING BUCKTAILS IN A LAKE FOR BASS

A MICKEY FINN BUCKTAIL (ABOVE), RED AND WHITE, GREY, YELLOW, BROWN AND BLACK BUCKTAILS OR STREAMERS ARE PREFERED IN SIZES 2 OR 4 ALTHOUGH OTHER SIZES MAY BE USED.

IF FLOATING BASS BUGS ARE UNPRODUCTIVE, TRY FIRST THE 5 TO 20 FT. DEPTHS WITH ANY OF THE ABOVE FLIES, USING SPLIT SHOT IF NEEDED TO SINK IT, LEADER AND LINE TO THE BOTTOM. TRY ALONG THE SHORE FIRST THEN FARTHER OUT WITH LONG CASTS (TORPEDO LINE IS BEST HERE). WAIT UNTIL IT SINKS THEN BEGIN THE SLOW RETRIEVE.

40 TO 70 FT.

RISKING WET FLIES BUT CATCHING BASS

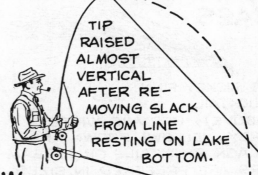

TIP RAISED ALMOST VERTICAL AFTER RE-MOVING SLACK FROM LINE RESTING ON LAKE BOTTOM.

WHEN DEEPLY SUNKEN BUCKTAILS ARE RESISTED BY BASS ON A SLOW, STEADY RETRIEVE, A SURE FIRE TRICK WAKES THEM. THE FLY MUST BE ON THE BOTTOM WITHOUT A SINKER IF POSSIBLE. REMOVE SLACK LINE WITH ROD TIP DOWN THEN SWEEP UPWARD IN A STEADY, <u>NOT FAST</u> ACTION. IF A BASS DOESN'T STRIKE DURING THE RAISE, ALLOW FLY TO SINK AGAIN BEFORE REPEATING.

FLY'S PATH OF ACTION

FLY SNAGS EASILY BUT <u>CATCHES FISH</u>!

TROLLING IN DEEP LAKES FOR BASS

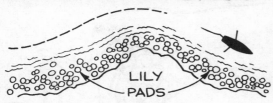

LILY
PADS

Chapter 8

Fishing
for Bass,
Pike, and
Other Pan
Fish

OARSMAN ROWS <u>VERY</u> SLOWLY
AND QUIETLY (OIL OARLOCKS TO
AVOID SQUEAKING!) TO TROLL
JUST BEYOND LILY PADS AND
SUBMERGED WEEDS IN STEEP
PITCH-OFFS PARALLEL TO SHORE
DURING HOT WEATHER. DAWN TO
MID-MORNING AND SUNSET-TO-DARK
ARE BEST FISHING HOURS.

USE
DEEP-
RUNNING
METAL LURES SUCH AS
A SILVER MINNOW WITH PORK RIND
STRIP (TOP) OR WIGGLER (BELOW).
REVERSE RUBBER SKIRT ON WIG-
GLER FOR BEST ACTION. SMALL,
DEEP-RUNNING PLUGS MAY ALSO
BE USED BY CLAMPING ENOUGH
SIZE 7 SPLIT SHOT 2-FT. ABOVE
LURE TO SINK IT TO THE BOTTOM.

151

LANDING A BASS WITHOUT A NET....

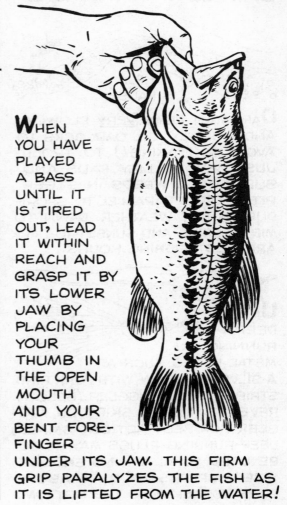

WHEN YOU HAVE PLAYED A BASS UNTIL IT IS TIRED OUT, LEAD IT WITHIN REACH AND GRASP IT BY ITS LOWER JAW BY PLACING YOUR THUMB IN THE OPEN MOUTH AND YOUR BENT FORE-FINGER UNDER ITS JAW. THIS FIRM GRIP PARALYZES THE FISH AS IT IS LIFTED FROM THE WATER!

152

MUSKIES AND PIKE

Chapter 8

Fishing
for Bass,
Pike, and
Other Pan
Fish

THESE FISH CLAMP AN ARTI-
FICIAL LURE CROSSWISE IN
THEIR HARD MOUTHS. THERE-
FORE, A <u>HARD</u> <u>STRIKE</u> IS NEC-
ESSARY TO PULL THE PLUG
THROUGH THEIR SHARP TEETH
(TO SINK THE HOOK DEEP IN THE
BONY MOUTH).

MOST BASS FISHERMEN, TRY-
ING FOR THESE FISH FOR THE
FIRST TIME, USUALLY STRIKE
SOFT AND MISS THEIR PRIZE.

RETRIEVE OR TROLL A PLUG
FASTER THAN YOU WOULD FOR
BASS OR WALLEYES TO GET
THEM TO STRIKE THE LURE.

SHORTER, STIFFER RODS ARE
USED INSTEAD OF THE REG-
ULAR BASS ROD TO HELP SET
THE SHARP HOOKS BEST.

153

WALLEYE TIPS.....

Chapter 8

Fishing
for Bass,
Pike, and
Other Pan
Fish

FOR THOSE WHO MAY
BE PLANNING A TRIP
INTO WALLEYE
TERRITORY
EXTENDING
THROUGH
MOST
OF

THE U.S.A.
INTO CANADA,
EXCEPT IN
THE FAR WEST
AND DEEP
SOUTH.

TROLL A SPOON, MIN-
NOW OR NIGHT-CRAWLER WITH A
SPINNER COMBINATION NEAR
SHORE AT DAWN AND DUSK.
IN HOT WEATHER THEY'LL BE
IN DEEP WATER AT NOON. IT'S
A SCHOOL FISH, SO WHERE ONE
IS HOOKED OTHERS MAY BE
FOUND ALSO. THE LARGEST
ARE CAUGHT AFTER DARK.

AT EVENING, SCHOOLS OF
WALLEYES HERD THE MINNOWS
INTO THE SHALLOW INLETS TO
FEED UPON. GOOD FISHING!

154

YELLOW PERCH TIPS

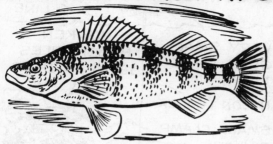

Chapter 8

Fishing
for Bass,
Pike, and
Other Pan
Fish

YELLOW OR RINGED PERCH RANGES MOST OF THE U.S.A. AND SOUTHERN CANADA AS SCHOOL FISH IN SLOW STREAMS OR LAKES.

AVERAGING LESS THAN A POUND, A SIZE 6 OR SMALLER HOOK IS BEST IN BAIT FISHING FOR THEM. SMALL MINNOWS, WORMS, CRAWFISH, "HOPPERS", ETC. IN THAT ORDER, ARE THE BEST BAITS FISHED FROM 3 TO 30 OR MORE FT. IN STREAMS AND LAKES. USE A SMALL THIN QUILL FLOAT FOR A BOBBER AND QUICKLY SET THE HOOK AS THE FISH TAKES THE FLOAT UNDER.

BAITING FOR CRAPPIE

LINE

VERY SMALL
QUILL TYPE
FLOAT

SUNKEN
BRUSH PILES
15' TO 30' DEEP.

NYLON LEADER

SMALL CLAMP
SINKER
18" ABOVE
#6 OR #8
HOOK.
1½" TO 2"
MINNOW

Chapter 8

Fishing
for Bass,
Pike, and
Other Pan
Fish

IN LAKES,
ANCHOR ABOVE BRUSH SHEL-
TERS TO STILL FISH WITH BAIT.
MINNOWS ARE THE FIRST CHOICE
FOLLOWED BY WORMS, GRASS-
HOPPERS, ETC.

WHEN FISH TAKES MINNOW, IT
MAY SWIM AWAY LIKE A BASS
BEFORE SWALLOWING IT OR IT
MAY EXPEL IT QUICKLY. IF A
DELAYED STRIKE IS MISSED,
STRIKE SOONER NEXT TIME.

SOFT MOUTHED, HOOK 'EM EASY!

156

ARTIFICIAL LURES FOR CRAPPIES.....

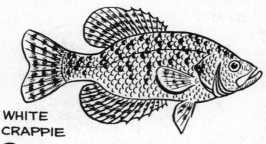

WHITE
CRAPPIE

Chapter 8

Fishing
for Bass,
Pike, and
Other Pan
Fish

SPINNING TACKLE LURES OF ALL TYPES, FROM ⅛ TO ¼ OZ., CAST NEAR UNDERWATER WEED BEDS AND BRUSH SHELTERS ARE A "NATURAL" FOR CRAPPIES. OR, USE A FLY ROD WITH WET FLIES IN SIZES FROM 4 TO 10. LET A FLY SINK THEN USE A HAND TWIST RETRIEVE. SPINNERS AND MIDGET BAIT CASTING LURES, AS WELL AS ABOVE LURES, CAN BE TROLLED. WORK ALL LURES VERY SLOWLY.

STRIKE <u>GENTLY</u> TO AVOID TEAR-ING HOOK OUT OF A CRAPPIE'S SOFT MOUTH.

157

BULLHEADS ON A WORM-BALL . . . . . .

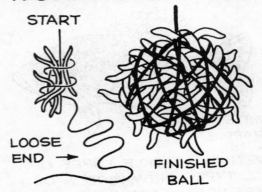

START

LOOSE END →

FINISHED BALL

START WORM BALL BY BINDING A FEW WORMS ON YOUR FISHING LINE WITH ITS LOOSE END AS SHOWN AT LEFT, ABOVE. KEEP ADDING AND BINDING A FEW AT A TIME UNTIL YOU'VE BOUND 50 OR SO WORMS INTO A COMPACT, SQUIRMING BALL.

ANCHOR YOUR BOAT OVER A LIKELY AREA AND PERMIT THE BALL TO SINK. IF LOCATION IS RIGHT A BULLHEAD WILL SOON GRAB THE BALL. RAISED GENTLY, THE CATFISH WILL BE RELUCTANT TO RELEASE ITS GRASP ON THE WORM BALL UNTIL IT'S IN THE BOAT. REPEATED USAGE WILL CATCH SEVERAL BULLHEADS.

DOUGH BAIT TIPS FOR CARP FISHING

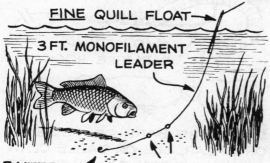

FINE QUILL FLOAT

3 FT. MONOFILAMENT LEADER

BAITED HOOK

2 SMALL SPLIT SHOT SINKERS

WRAP SLICES OF OLD BREAD IN A CLOTH TO SOAK IN WATER. THEN SQUEEZE WATER OUT, UNWRAP AND KNEAD THE DOUGH WHILE ADDING A LITTLE CORNMEAL. TOO MUCH MEAL MAKES IT BRITTLE. WHEN FIRM, IT'S DONE. COVER A NO. 2 SPROAT HOOK'S BEND AND BARB ONLY WITH A PINCH OF DOUGH. IF STRIKES ARE MISSED, COVER THE BARB ONLY. IF WATER IS WEEDY, CLEAR A SPACE TO FISH ON THE BOTTOM. USE 12 FT. CANE POLE OR 9 FT. STIFF FLY ROD WITH SHORT LINE. STRIKE AT SLIGHTEST ACTION OF FLOAT, INSTANTLY!

1ST   2ND

159

SUCKER FISHING...

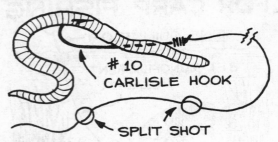

#10
CARLISLE HOOK

SPLIT SHOT

Chapter 8

Fishing
for Bass,
Pike, and
Other Pan
Fish

BURY THE BARB OF A SIZE 8
OR 10 CARLISLE OR EAGLE CLAW
HOOK IN A WORM FOR BAIT. USE
A NYLON LEADER AND SPLIT
SHOT (JUST ENOUGH TO SINK)
ABOUT 12" TO 18" ABOVE WORM.
FISH DEEP WITH A FLY ROD OR
CANE POLE IN POOLS, UNDER A
BANK, ETC. TROUT-LIKE.

"SNATCH-FISHING" IS VERY POP-
ULAR IN SOME STATES WHERE
IT IS LEGAL. BE SURE IT'S LEGAL
BEFORE USING THIS METHOD. IF
THE STREAM-BED IS GRAVEL OR
SAND, USE A DIPSEY SINKER ON
THE END. IF IT'S ROCKY, PLACE
SINKER ABOVE HOOKS. TIE 12
LARGE CLAW HOOKS 4" APART
AS SHOWN. WHEN YOU SEE FISH
PASS OVER SUNKEN LINE, JERK
QUICKLY TO FOUL HOOK THEM.

TACKLE BUSTING ALLIGATOR GARS!

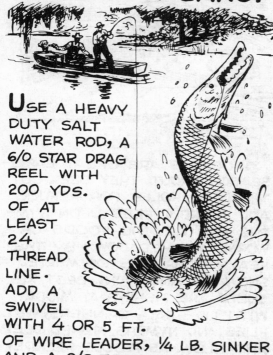

USE A HEAVY DUTY SALT WATER ROD, A 6/0 STAR DRAG REEL WITH 200 YDS. OF AT LEAST 24 THREAD LINE. ADD A SWIVEL WITH 4 OR 5 FT. OF WIRE LEADER, ¼ LB. SINKER AND A 9/0 TREBLE HOOK.

AFTER SEVERAL SPECTACULAR RUNS IT WILL BE NECESSARY TO FINALLY SHOOT THE GAR BECAUSE HIS TOUGH SKIN IS OTHERWISE DIFFICULT TO PENETRATE. IT IS NOT EXPENSIVE SPORT FISHING WITH A NATIVE GUIDE FOR YOUR INSTRUCTOR!

BROOK TROUT TIPS

"BROOKIES" ARE GREAT EARLY-SEASON TROUT. THEY SEEK OUT THE DEEP HOLES FOR REFUGE AND THEREIN FEED UPON NYMPHS AND AQUATIC FOODS OR WORMS WASHED DOWN BY THE HEAVY TORRENTS OF MELTED SNOW, ICE AND RAIN. BEST RESULTS ARE FISHING AT MIDDAY WITH LIVE BAIT, SPINNERS, WET FLIES AND NYMPHS FISHED DEEP AND SLOW. AS FLOODS RECEDE, AND THE WATER WARMS TO 50°, BROOKIES MOVE ABOUT MORE FREELY, FEEDING AT MID MORNING AND AFTERNOON. KEEP FISHING DEEP!

162

BROOK TROUT TIPS... WARMER WATER TEMPERATURES

AT 60° WATER TEMPERATURE, THE TROUT BEGIN TO FEED HEAVILY ON SURFACE FLIES TOWARD EVENING. MORNING MAY PRODUCE ALSO. CONTRARY TO POPULAR BELIEF, "BROOKIES" AREN'T AS CAUTIOUS AS OTHER TROUT FOR <u>THEY</u> WILL TAKE ARTIFICIALS SUCH AS THIS FLY WHICH RESEMBLES NO <u>TRUE</u> FLY, THUS ENDEARING THEM TO FLY-ROD MEN.

THE "PARMACHENE BELLE"

163

STREAM SIGNS FOR TROUT........

CURRENT

IN SHALLOW STREAMS, A DARK PATCH OF WATER SURROUNDED BY LIGHTER COLORED WATER INDICATES A HOLE WHERE THE CURRENT LESSENS TO HARBOR A TROUT. SUBMERGED BOULDERS CAUSE FOAM OR BROKEN SURFACE WATERS ABOVE THEM. THE CURRENT GOUGES OUT HOLES BEFORE AND AFTER BOULDERS THAT PROVIDE COVER AND REST AGAINST A STREAM'S FORCE.

TROUT SELDOM EXPOSE THEMSELVES IN DAYLIGHT. FISH THE FASTER, BROKEN WATER AND ALONG THE EDGE OF THE MAIN CURRENT WHERE A NATURAL COVER IS PROVIDED. FISH REST IN THE SLOWER EDGES WHERE THEY CAN DART INTO THE MAIN CHANNEL FOR PASSING FOOD.

164

"TAILING" AND "BULGING" TROUT

CURRENT

A TROUT'S TAIL PROTRUDING
ABOVE THE WATER'S SURFACE
IN MEDIUM-FAST WATER OF A
SHALLOW RUN MEANS: FEED-
ING DEEP ON DRIFTING NYMPHS,
BEFORE FLY-HATCH BEGINS. FISH
WITH 2 OR 3 LIVE OR IMITATION
NYMPHS, WEIGHTED TO DRIFT
DEEP.

BULGING OCCURS
AS NYMPHS RISE TO SURFACE TO
HATCH IN CALMER WATERS. FIN
OR SWIRLED WATER IS TIP-OFF.
FISH DRIFTED NYMPH OR WET FLY.

165

STRIKING TROUT WITH A DRY FLY...

MOST DRY-
FLY ANGLERS
STRIKE TOO
SOON!

EXPERIMENTS
HAVE PROVED
THAT WHEN
UNATTACHED ARTI-
FICIAL FLIES WERE THROWN
INTO A POOL, TROUT TOOK
THEM TO THE BOTTOM BEFORE
SPITTING THEM OUT. THUS, A
TIED-ON FLY IS TAKEN ALSO IF
THE LINE IS NOT RESISTANT!
SMALL TROUT TAKE QUICKER
THAN LARGE ONES. MOST BIG
TROUT ARE MISSED BECAUSE
ANGLERS STRIKE TOO QUICKLY.

IN QUIET POOLS THE STRIKE
IS SLOWER THAN IN FAST WATER!

166

WHICH FLY PATTERN SHALL YOU USE?

TRY TO MATCH THE FLIES THE FISH ARE FEEDING ON.

EARLY-SEASON WATERS MAY BE SPRING RUN-OFFS OR FLOOD-LIKE SO USE LARGER THAN NORMAL SIZES OF DARK COLORS, PERHAPS WITH A SPINNER, DISTINGUISHING IT FROM WASH-OUT DEBRIS. FISH <u>DEEP</u>!

NEAR DARKNESS OF EVENING, LARGER FAN OR SPENT WING DRY FLIES WORK WELL IF THE WATER IS WARMING UP. MORE VISIBILITY IN RIFFLES, TOO.

IF YOU MISS ON A STRIKE AND FISH QUIT YOUR OFFERINGS, SWITCH TO A SMALLER FLY.

QUICK SWITCH TO A DIFFERENT DRY FLY MAY BRING STRIKES

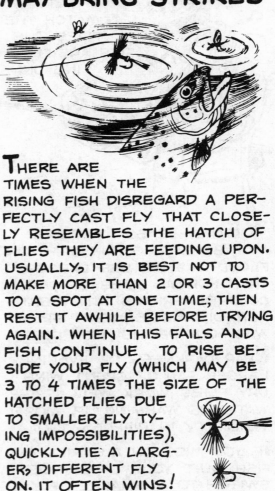

THERE ARE TIMES WHEN THE RISING FISH DISREGARD A PERFECTLY CAST FLY THAT CLOSELY RESEMBLES THE HATCH OF FLIES THEY ARE FEEDING UPON. USUALLY, IT IS BEST NOT TO MAKE MORE THAN 2 OR 3 CASTS TO A SPOT AT ONE TIME; THEN REST IT AWHILE BEFORE TRYING AGAIN. WHEN THIS FAILS AND FISH CONTINUE TO RISE BESIDE YOUR FLY (WHICH MAY BE 3 TO 4 TIMES THE SIZE OF THE HATCHED FLIES DUE TO SMALLER FLY TYING IMPOSSIBILITIES), QUICKLY TIE A LARGER, DIFFERENT FLY ON. IT OFTEN WINS!

FISHING THE RIFFLES

CURRENT

EARLY MORN AND TOWARDS EVENING, TROUT AND SMALL MOUTH BASS MAY BE FOUND IN SHALLOW RIFFLES. A LONG CAST IS NOT NEEDED BECAUSE THE BROKEN SURFACE OF THE WATER REDUCES THE FISHES' VISIBILITY. BEGINNERS NEED USE ONLY 10 TO 15 FT. OF LINE WITH A 9 FT. LEADER. HIGHLY VISIBLE, A PARTLY WHITE BIVISIBLE DRY FLY IS IDEAL, OR USE A WET FLY OR STREAMER. WHEN YOUR FLY DISAPPEARS, "STRIKE" SOFTLY, BUT QUICKLY.

169

FLY FISHING THE QUIET STRETCHES

GREEN DRAKE
DRY FLY

SOMETIMES A DRY FLY OR BUG WILL FRIGHTEN TROUT IN SUCH WATERS. WHEN THIS HAPPENS MAKE A QUICK SWITCH TO A NYMPH OR WET FLY.

LET FLY SINK SLOWLY TO THE BOTTOM. THE ALARMED FISH WILL QUIET DOWN AS THEY SEE IT SINK WITHOUT HARM AND BECOMING CURIOUS, WILL INVESTIGATE IT CLOSER, PERHAPS PICK IT UP!

IF THEY DON'T, GENTLY LIFT IT OFF THE BOTTOM AND TWITCH IT WITH A HAND-TWIST RETRIEVE.

170

USING AN IMITATION STONE FLY.........

STREAM BASS AND TROUT FEED HEAVILY ON NYMPHS AND ADULTS ALIKE WHEREEVER THEY ARE FOUND.

A GOOD IMITATION SUCH AS THAT SHOWN ABOVE MAY BE FLY CAST AGAINST A LARGE BOULDER BEFORE FALLING INTO THE WATER TO BE TAKEN BY A HIDING FISH LYING IN WAIT FOR AN EASY MORSEL. THIS FLY IS MADE TO SINK RAPIDLY, THE CURRENT GIVING IT ACTION. USUALLY, THE STRIKE COMES SOON AFTER IT HITS THE WATER.

171

USING NYMPHS FOR SPRING FISHING....

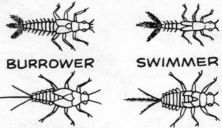

BURROWER   SWIMMER

CLAMBERER   CLINGER

MAY FLY NYMPHS ARE DIVIDED INTO 4 TYPES. EACH IS SHOWN ABOVE, ITS NAME DESCRIBING ITS STREAM MANNERS. EACH RISES IN THE STREAM TO SHED ITS SHUCK, BECOMING A DUN FLY IN MATURITY.

IN COOLER SPRING WEATHER, BE-FORE THE FIRST MAY FLIES HATCH, THESE AND OTHER NYMPHS ARE DISLODGED BY HEAVY CURRENTS AS ROCKS ARE TUMBLED IN THE STREAM. THE NYMPHS ARE WASH-ED ALONG THE STREAM BOTTOM WHERE TROUT ARE WAITING FOR THEM. KEEP YOUR IMITATION NYMPH ON THE BOTTOM, BOUNC-ING AGAINST ROCKS, INTO HOLES, ETC. STRIKE WHEN YOU FEEL A TUG OR LINE ACTS STRANGELY.

172

FLY-FISHING TIP...

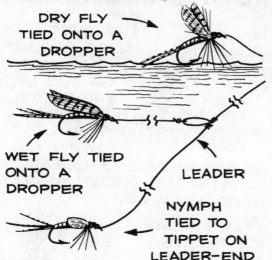

DRY FLY TIED ONTO A DROPPER

WET FLY TIED ONTO A DROPPER

LEADER

NYMPH TIED TO TIPPET ON LEADER-END

WHEN A HATCH OF FLIES HAS JUST STARTED, OR IS ON, TRY USING A NYMPH, WET FLY AND A DRY FLY, <u>ALL</u> <u>OF</u> <u>THE</u> <u>SAME</u> <u>PATTERN</u> TO IMITATE CHANGING PHASES OF THE HATCH FROM A STREAM-BED NYMPH TO THE DUN FLY READY TO TAKE WING. TIE NYMPH TO DRIFT DEEPER THAN THE WET FLY WHICH DRIFTS A FEW INCHES UNDER THE FLOATING DRY FLY. IT'S A NATURAL COMBINATION TO FEEDING FISH.

WHERE ONLY 2 FLIES ARE LEGAL, USE ANY 2 FOR A COMBINATION.

173

FLY FISHING TIPS...

GOOD

THE BEST DRY FLIES SHOULD FLOAT HIGH ON TOP OF THE WATER. THE "LEE WULFF" WITH ITS HEAVY HACKLE (AN IDEAL FLOATER) IS SHOWN AS A GOOD EXAMPLE.

WHEN A DRY FLY FLOATS LOW IN THE WATER, DIP IT IN DRY FLY OIL TO RESTORE ITS FLOATING QUALITIES.

BAD

THE COILING TENDENCY OF NYLON LEADER MATERIAL MAY BE REMOVED SO IT WILL LAY OUT STRAIGHT AFTER CASTING BY RUBBING IT BRISKLY WITH A SMALL PIECE OF RUBBER INNER TUBE.

USING EXTRA WET FLIES FOR TROUT

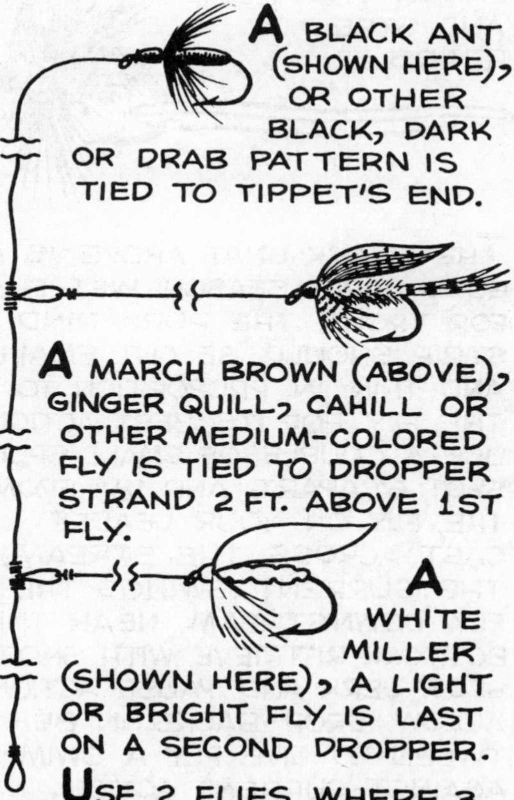

A BLACK ANT (SHOWN HERE), OR OTHER BLACK, DARK OR DRAB PATTERN IS TIED TO TIPPET'S END.

A MARCH BROWN (ABOVE), GINGER QUILL, CAHILL OR OTHER MEDIUM-COLORED FLY IS TIED TO DROPPER STRAND 2 FT. ABOVE 1ST FLY.

A WHITE MILLER (SHOWN HERE), A LIGHT OR BRIGHT FLY IS LAST ON A SECOND DROPPER.

USE 2 FLIES WHERE 3 ARE ILLEGAL. THUS, IT'S FASTER TO FIND THE FISHES' PREFERRED FLY. TOP FLY MAY BE LARGE TO BE AN ATTRACTOR IN FASTER CURRENTS.

175

A PORK RIND FLY TIP FOR LARGE TROUT AND STEEL-HEADS

THE BLACK GNAT ABOVE IS A GOOD EARLY SEASON WET FLY FOR TROUT. THE PORK RIND STRIP SHOULD BE CUT SMALL AND THIN IN PROPORTION TO THE FLY FOR ITS BEST ACTION. USE A COUPLE OF SMALL SPLIT SHOT 6" APART, AND 18" FROM THE FLY ON YOUR LEADER. CAST ACROSS THE STREAM, THE CURRENT SWINGS THE FLY DOWNSTREAM NEAR THE BOTTOM. RETRIEVE WITH SHORT SLOW JERK AND PAUSE ACTION, ALLOW DROP-BACKS IN BE-TWEEN TO GIVE FLY A SWIM-AGAINST-CURRENT ACTION.

THE "GLORY" STREAMER FLY

176

PLUGS FOR TROUT?

NOT MANY ANGLERS REALIZE
THAT LARGER
TROUT <u>WILL</u>
TAKE A
PLUG OR
SPOON!

SMALL TROUT FEED MAINLY
ON INSECTS, WORMS, MINNOWS,
ETC. <u>LARGE</u> TROUT HAVE HUGE
APPETITES TO SUIT THEIR SIZE
SO THEY'RE USUALLY LOOKING
FOR LARGER PREY. MOST ANG-
LERS KNOW THAT <u>LARGER</u> TROUT
ARE CAUGHT ON LARGE MINNOWS
BUT THEY NEVER THINK OF TRY-
ING A PLUG SUCH AS FOR BASS.
LARGE SPOONS ARE GOOD ALSO.
TROUT HAVE ALWAYS BEEN
ASSOCIATED WITH FLIES, ETC.
IT'S GOOD TO TRY BASS TRICKS
FOR TROUT AND VICE-VERSA IF
YOU REALLY WANT TO <u>CATCH</u> FISH.

177

USING STREAMERS AND BUCKTAILS FOR LARGE TROUT

LARGE TROUT SEEK THE QUIET, DEEP HOLES BELOW FASTER FEED-LANES <u>DURING</u> <u>THE</u> <u>DAY</u> WHERE THEY HARDLY MOVE A FIN IN REST. DRIFT THE LURE DEEP IN THESE POOLS AND LET THE CURRENT MOVE IT AROUND AT WILL. DON'T BE IN A HURRY TO RETRIEVE IT. A LARGE TROUT MAY WATCH IT QUITE AWHILE BEFORE DECIDING IT'S A SAFE BITE.

IN LATE AFTERNOON THE LARGE TROUT MOVE UP INTO THE FEED-LANES. DRIFT LURE DOWNSTREAM ON A TAUT LINE TO DART TO-AND-FRO IN THE CURRENTS WITHOUT FREQUENT RETRIEVES.

178

LARGE TROUT LURES

SPINNER
AND FLY

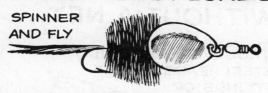

SPOON

RED AND WHITE SPOONS USED
FOR PIKE, BASS AND PACIFIC
SALMON IN THE PAST ARE DEAD-
LY ON LARGE TROUT. A 2½ INCH
SPOON IS CAST WITH A BAIT CAST-
ING ROD ACROSS WIDE STREAMS
THAT FLY RODS CAN'T REACH.
REPLACE TREBLE HOOKS WITH A
LARGER SINGLE HOOK. IT SNAGS
LESS AND HOOKS WELL. QUIETLY
CAST LURE UPSTREAM FROM FISH,
LETTING IT FLUTTER AND TUMBLE
TO DRIFT INTO HOLE ON A SEMI-
TAUT LINE. THUS, TROUT OFTEN
HOOK THEMSELVES IN STRIKING.

A BRONZE SPINNER WITH A
BROWN PALMER FLY ON A DROP-
PER AND A DIPSEY SINKER ON A
LEADER'S END IS FISHED THE
SAME. IT IMITATES A SCULPIN OR
BROAD-HEADED MINNOW.

LAND LARGE FISH WITHOUT A NET....

TROUT, SALMON AND STEELHEADS OF FIVE POUNDS OR MORE...

...CAN BE BEACHED ON A SELECTED GENTLY SLOPED SAND BAR OR GRAVELED BANK. WAIT UNTIL THE PLAYED-OUT TROPHY TURNS ON HIS SIDE. LEAD HIM IN OVER THE WATER'S SURFACE, SLIDING HIM ONTO THE SHORE WITHOUT STOPPING. STAND BACK FROM THE FISH SO THE STRAIN IS ON THE ROD'S HEAVY SECTION AND NOT ITS TIP!

OR, GENTLY SLIDE...

...YOUR HAND ALONG THE BACK OF A TIRED TROUT (LYING ON ITS SIDE). WHEN THUMB AND INDEX FINGER REST ON BACK EDGE OF GILL COVERS, GRIP HARD WITH THEM AND LIFT THE PRIZE.

BAIT—HOW TO
GET AND USE IT

For a busy man the easiest way to get bait is to buy it. However, in some states minnows and other live bait cannot be sold.

During warm summer months when garden worms have gone very deep in the earth, it's best to buy worms, if you don't raise them, instead of digging barren ground. Or, you might sprinkle your lawn and try for "night crawlers."

Try to present your bait to the fish as though it were free of your restraining line and leader.

Hatchery-reared fish that have recently been stocked into lakes and streams are less selective than native wild fish. It's wise to use a leader as fine as conditions will allow for either fish. Use just enough sinker weight to carry your bait down to the fish. For best results a sinker should not be used unless it is absolutely necessary.

Fish are most often caught on bait normally found in their native waters. However, it sometimes pays to use something different.

COLLECTING NIGHT CRAWLERS IS EASY!

A NIGHT
CRAWLER
EMERGING
FROM ITS HOLE

NIGHT CRAWLERS, KNOWN
ALSO AS NIGHT WALKERS,
ARE LARGE WORMS, PENCIL
THICK AND 4 TO 8 INCHES IN
LENGTH. THEY ARE EXCELLENT
BAIT FOR FRESH WATER FISH.

MOIST AND LIGHT-SHY, THEY
DO EMERGE ON DEWY NIGHTS,
OR AFTER A HEAVY RAIN.

STIR ¼ CAN OF DRY MUSTARD
IN 2 QTS. OF WATER. A BIT OF
THIS IN THE HOLES BRINGS 'EM
UP! RINSE ALL WORMS CARE-
FULLY IN FRESH WATER.

HOW TO CATCH
"NIGHT CRAWLERS"

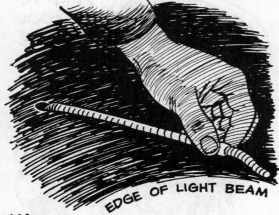

EDGE OF LIGHT BEAM

WHEN GATHERING NIGHT CRAWLERS
OR DEW WORMS AT NIGHT, MOVE
YOUR LIGHT SLOWLY AND LOCATE
WORMS AT ITS EDGE. DON'T PUT A
LIGHT DIRECTLY ON THE WORM.
TURN THE LIGHT OFF WHEN YOU
GRASP A WORM SO OTHERS NEARBY
WILL NOT BE FRIGHTENED AWAY.
USE WET DIRT ON YOUR FINGERS
TO HOLD THE WORM BETTER AS IT
CONTRACTS ITS BODY WHEN YOU
GRASP IT. A WORM USUALLY HAS
ITS TAIL IN A HOLE TO PULL WITH.
DON'T PULL OR YOU'LL YANK IT
IN TWO. JUST HOLD ON AND THE
WORM WILL SOON RELAX. PULL
ONLY BETWEEN CONTRACTIONS.

WORM CARRIERS

KEEP IN
A COOL
PLACE

CREEL

MANUFACTURED CORK CON-
TAINERS THAT KEEP WORMS
LIVELY FOR SEVERAL DAYS
MAY BE PURCHASED IN TACKLE
STORES. OR, YOUR WILLOW
CREEL MAY BE USED TO TRANS-
PORT WORMS IN TO CAMP.
PACK THE CREEL WITH WOODS
MOSS (WITHOUT MUCH GRIT),
THEN DUMP ABOUT 50 WORMS
ON TOP. WHEN THEY HAVE DIS-
APPEARED INTO THE MOSS, ADD
ANOTHER 50. REPEAT UNTIL FULL.
DISCARD THOSE NOT DISAPPEARING.

"GARDEN HACKLE" OR ANGLE WORMS

For the novice or inexpert, nothing will take trout or other early season fresh water fish faster than a common garden worm otherwise called "garden hackle" in fishing circles.

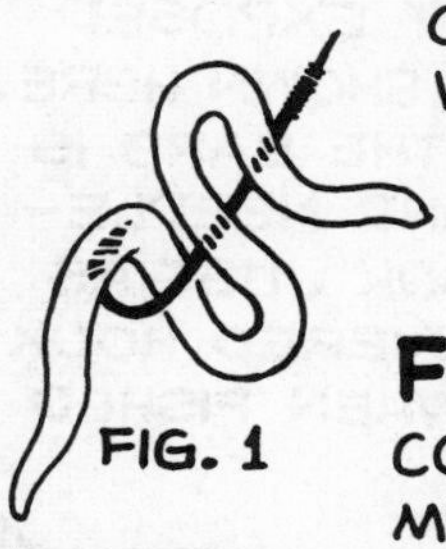

FIG. 1

Figure 1 shows a common hooking method. The barb is buried in the worm.

Figure 2 shows a "threading" technique. This gives good action and is ideal for larger worms.

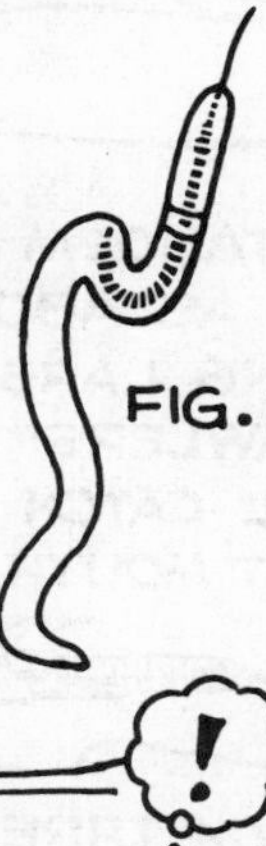

FIG. 2

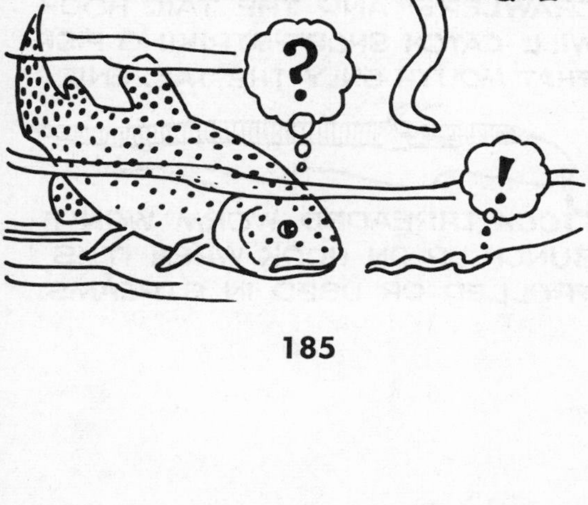

HOOKING OF WORMS

SOME ANGLERS CLAIM IT'S HARDER TO SET A HOOK'S BARB DEEP IN A FISH IF THE BARB IS NOT EXPOSED AS SHOWN HERE. IF THE BARB IS WORM COVERED AND NEEDLE-SHARP IT WILL HOOK JUST AS WELL. A BARB-COVERED HOOK WILL SNAG LESS WHEN FISHED ON THE BOTTOM.

A TANDEM OR GANG-HOOKING RIG AS ABOVE IS IDEAL WHEN USING LARGE WORMS OR "NIGHT-CRAWLERS" AND THE TAIL HOOK WILL CATCH SHORT-STRIKING FISH THAT MOUTH ONLY THE TAIL END.

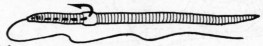

HOOK-THREADED WORM WON'T BUNCH UP ON HOOK WHEN IT IS TROLLED OR USED IN STREAMS.

186

USE DIPSY SINKERS TO SAVE WORMS

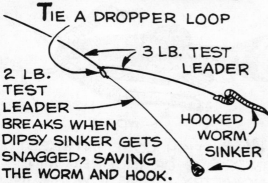

TIE A DROPPER LOOP

3 LB. TEST LEADER

2 LB. TEST LEADER BREAKS WHEN DIPSY SINKER GETS SNAGGED, SAVING THE WORM AND HOOK.

HOOKED WORM

SINKER

IN FAST WATER IT IS NECESSARY TO USE A SINKER TO GET A WORM DEEP ENOUGH TO REACH BOTTOM FEEDING FISH. THE RIG SHOWN ABOVE IS IDEAL FOR THIS. USE A SINKER THAT IS <u>JUST</u> HEAVY ENOUGH TO TAKE IT DOWN, OTHERWISE IT WILL SNAG AT ONCE.

PLAY OUT LINE FAST ENOUGH TO FEEL THE SINKER BUMPING THE BOTTOM BUT NOT HALTING. WHEN YOU GET THE "FEEL" OF DANGEROUS SNAGS, A QUICK PULL MAY PREVENT LOSS OF THE SINKER.

TRY A WORM OR A FLY WITH MINNOWS

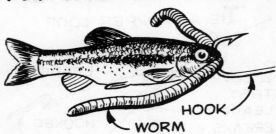

HOOK

WORM

WHEN FISH LOSE INTEREST IN A LIVE OR INJURED MIN- NOW, TRY FIXING A WORM IN THE MINNOW'S MOUTH WITH YOUR HOOK. THUS THE MIN- NOW LOOKS DOUBLY INTEREST- ING AS IT TUMBLES ALONG IN THE CURRENT.

STRAIGHT EYE

A FLY OR STREAMER HOOKED AS ABOVE IS A FAVORITE ALSO. USE WITH A STRAIGHT-EYED STREAMER FOR TROLLING. A SWIVEL BETWEEN LEADER AND LINE WITH A KEEL ON THE LINE PREVENTS TWISTING.

188

MINNOW TRAP TIPS

CURRENT

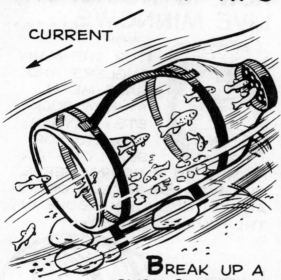

BREAK UP A SLICE OF BREAD TO USE FOR BAIT IN A TRAP AND SUBMERGE THE TRAP IN A SHALLOW STREAM WITH THE FUNNELED ENTRY DOWNSTREAM. THE BREAD FLAVORS THE WATER BELOW THE TRAP, LURING THE MINNOWS TO IT. SET THE TRAP AT NIGHT AND COLLECT THE MINNOWS IN THE MORNING.

UNKNOWN MINNOWS SHOULD NOT BE DUMPED WHERE YOU FISH BECAUSE YOU MIGHT BE PLANTING AN UNDESIRABLE SPECIES FROM OTHER WATERS.

HOW TO TRANSPORT LIVE MINNOWS......

For THE MANY ANGLERS WHO HAVE METAL MINNOW BUCKETS, OXYGEN TABLETS FOR SUPPLYING AIR FROM 5 TO 12 HOURS SERVE THE PURPOSE NICELY. ONE IN ACTION IS SHOWN ABOVE IN THE "CUT-AWAY" VIEW.

LATELY, LAMINATED FIBER PAPER MATERIAL, BREATHING AIR AS IT EVAPORATES WATER BUT DOESN'T LEAK, IS BEING USED FOR MINNOW BUCKETS IN SEVERAL MODELS, ONE OF WHICH IS SHOWN. THESE DURABLE BUCKETS KEEP MINNOWS ALIVE FOR DAYS WITHOUT CHANGING THE WATER.

190

MINNOW TIPS FOR THE BEGINNERS...

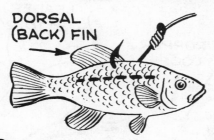

DORSAL (BACK) FIN

PLACE HOOK THROUGH TOP OF MINNOW'S BACK WHERE DORSAL FIN JOINS, FOR STILL FISHING. IN THIS METHOD THE MINNOW SWIMS FREELY AND LIVES LONGER.

DO NOT PLACE HOOK THROUGH BACKBONE (DOTTED LINE), IN BELLY OR HEAD. THIS KILLS MINNOW MOST QUICKLY.

USE SMALL SHOT WEIGHTS FIXED ON NYLON LEADER 18 INCHES FROM MINNOW TO CARRY IT DOWN DEEP WHERE FISH MAY BE FEEDING. ALLOW FISH TAKING MINNOW TWO "RUNS" OF SEVERAL FEET (FISH BEGINS TO SWALLOW MINNOW ON SECOND RUN) THEN "STRIKE" BY RAISING ROD TIP.

191

LIVE MINNOW RIG FOR STILL FISHING

LARGE CORK

LEADER 8" TO 12"

DROPPER LOOP

DIPSEY SINKER

SOME MINNOW SPECIES TRY TO SWIM DOWN INTO WEED BEDS TO HIDE FROM GAME FISH. PREVENT THIS WITH THIS RIG. TIE A DROPPER LOOP ABOVE WEEDS AND USE A CORK TO FLOAT THE MINNOW SO IT CAN BE SEEN TO LURE PROWLING GAME FISH.

192

INJURED MINNOWS ARE GOOD LURES!

It is instinctive for game fish to kill maimed or injured smaller fish and it is easier prey as well. This is the reason why such imitations in bait casting plugs, the tumbling spoons and sewn-on dead minnows are so effective if fished properly. A dead, sewed-on minnow, drifting with the stream flow is a killer for large trout and bass.

Streamer and bucktail wet flies have similar appeal when fished to imitate a weak minnow against a current.

193

HOW TO SEW A MINNOW ON A HOOK -FLY ROD FISHING-

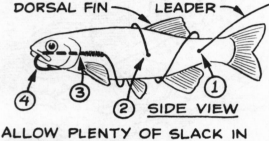

DORSAL FIN — LEADER —

SIDE VIEW

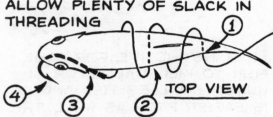

ALLOW PLENTY OF SLACK IN THREADING

TOP VIEW

A NUMBER 5 EYELESS HOOK WORKS BEST BUT AN EYED HOOK MAY BE USED WITH CARE. FIRST PASS IT THROUGH BETWEEN TAIL AND DORSAL FIN AT ①. THEN WRAP AND PIERCE AGAIN AT ②. WRAP A-GAIN THEN THREAD IT IN THE GILL ③ AND OUT THE CORNER OF THE MOUTH ④. REMOVE SLACK. WEIGHTED, THE DEAD BAIT IS CAST ACROSS THE CUR-RENT TO DRIFT DOWNSTREAM.

HOW TO SEW A MINNOW TO TROLL

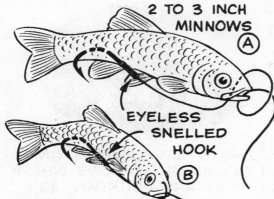

2 TO 3 INCH MINNOWS
(A)

EYELESS SNELLED HOOK
(B)

USE AN EYELESS HOOK LIKE A NEEDLE FOR THREADING. PASS THE HOOK THROUGH THE LOWER JAW FROM THE TOP THEN MAKE A LOOP BY PIERCING FROM TOP TO BOTTOM AS IN (A). NOW PASS HOOK INTO AND OUT OF THE SIDE. TIGHTEN LINE AND LOOP AS IN (B) SO THAT MINNOW IS SET IN A CURVE. THIS CURVE SPINS THE MINNOW IN TROLLING. A SWIVEL IS USED ON LINE TO PREVENT ITS TWIST.

TROLL AT 2 TO 3 MILES PER HOUR FOR WALLEYES, LANDLOCKED SALMON, LARGE TROUT, TOGUE, ETC.

195

EASILY CAUGHT GRASSHOPPERS...

USING A FLASHLIGHT AT NIGHT IN FIELDS OR MEADOWS WHERE HOPPERS ARE ABUNDANT IS THE BEST WAY TO CATCH THEM WITHOUT THE DAY-TIME CHASE.

COVER A QUART GLASS JAR BY TYING A PIECE OF RUBBER INNERTUBE HAVING AIR HOLES AND A SLIT IN IT FOR KEEPING YOUR BAIT AS SHOWN.

HOPPERS ARE EXCELLENT WARM WEATHER BAIT FOR FRESH WATER GAME FISH.

SLIT

196

HOW TO BAIT WITH GRASSHOPPERS.....

FOR BASS AND TROUT FISH-
ING RUN THE HOOK LENGTH-
WISE FROM HEAD TO TAIL. A
HOPPER IS NOT SO EASILY
LOST WHEN SO HOOKED.

FOR PAN FISH SUCH AS
SUNFISH, PERCH, ROCK BASS,
ETC., REMOVE THE HOPPER'S
WINGS AND LEGS AFTER
HOOKING AS ABOVE.

USE A NUMBER 6 HOOK FOR
BASS OR TROUT OR A NO. 8
HOOK FOR PAN FISH.

IN STREAM FISHING, IT MAY
BE NECESSARY TO USE ONE
OR TWO SMALL SPLIT SHOT
IF THE FISH ARE DEEP.

197

HOOK FOR A LIVE GRASSHOPPER....

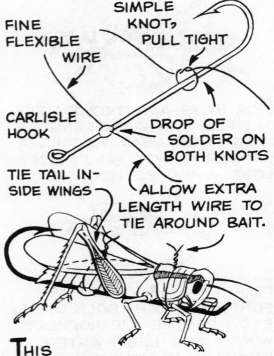

FINE
FLEXIBLE
WIRE

SIMPLE
KNOT,
PULL TIGHT

CARLISLE
HOOK

DROP OF
SOLDER ON
BOTH KNOTS

TIE TAIL IN-
SIDE WINGS

ALLOW EXTRA
LENGTH WIRE TO
TIE AROUND BAIT.

THIS
EASILY MADE TIE-ON HOOK IS
USED FOR LIVE STONE FLY
NYMPHS, CRICKETS, ETC. ALSO.
SELECT HOOK SIZES ACCORD-
ING TO INSECTS USED AND
WHAT FISH YOU'RE AFTER.

USE AFTER A HOPPER DRIVE, ON
A FLY ROD. NOT SO EASILY LOST!

198

SMALLMOUTH BASS GO FOR CRICKETS!

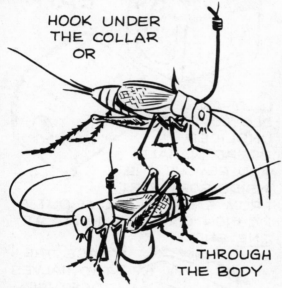

HOOK UNDER
THE COLLAR
OR

THROUGH
THE BODY

CRICKETS ARE CONSIDERED BY SOME FISHERMEN TO BE THE <u>BEST</u> BAIT FOR SMALL-MOUTHS.

PUNCH HOLES FOR VENTILATION IN THE COVER OF A GLASS FRUIT JAR TO CARRY CRICKETS IN. HOOK CAREFULLY AND CAST GENTLY TO AVOID FLIPPING THEM OFF THE HOOK, OR JUST LOW-ER THEM INTO THE WATER WITH SPLIT SHOT FOR WEIGHT.

TRAPPING CRICKETS FOR BAIT

Cut an old loaf of unsliced bread in half and remove the inside soft part from each half. Cut out a 1½ inch circular hole at one end.

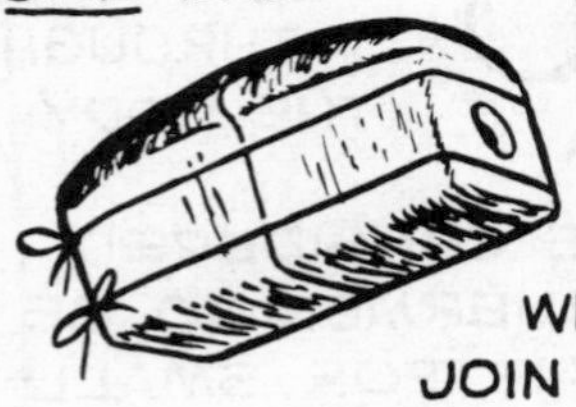

HOLE

Place the two halves together, tying them with string or join with rubber bands.

Leave it in high grass (the night before you go fishing) to catch the crickets. Shake them out through the hole into a fruit jar.

200

CRAYFISH, CRAWFISH, CRAWDADS OR CRABS

THIS POPULAR VARIOUS-NAMED BAIT IS FOUND IN ROCKY SHALLOWS ON MOSSY STRETCHES OF STREAMS. HAVE YOUR PAL HOLD A SEINE OR WIRE SCREEN DOWNSTREAM TO CATCH THEM AS YOU TURN OVER THE ROCKS SHELTERING THEM. THE YOUNG GROW FAST IN WARM WEATHER, SHEDDING HARD SHELLS FOR SOFT SEVERAL TIMES. THESE LIGHT CRAWFISH ARE CHOICE BAIT FOR MOST FRESH WATER GAME FISH.

HOOK LIVE CRAWFISH OR TAIL AS SHOWN.

CRAWFISH RIG INSURES HOOKING

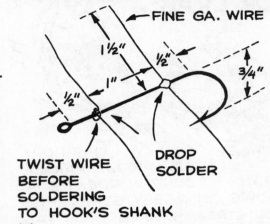

FINE GA. WIRE

1½"

½"

¾"

1"

½"

TWIST WIRE
BEFORE
SOLDERING
TO HOOK'S SHANK

DROP
SOLDER

USE HOOKS WITH A 2" SHANK
BEFORE BEND AND ¾" ACROSS
BEND FOR LARGER CRAWFISH
AS ABOVE. USE FINE, FLEXIBLE
WIRE, ENDS EXTENDING 1½" OFF
SHANK TO WRAP AND TWIST A-
ROUND CRAWFISH'S BODY. USE
SMALLER HOOKS FOR SMALL
CRAWFISH.

EXPOSING HOOK INSURES HOOKING

THIS RIG WON'T KILL THE BAIT!

BAIT FISHING IN LAKES WITH CRAWFISH

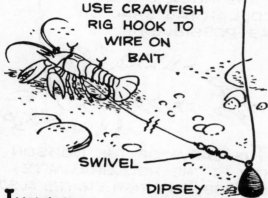

USE CRAWFISH RIG HOOK TO WIRE ON BAIT

SWIVEL

DIPSEY SINKER

IN LAKES, FISH NEAR UNDERWATER SPRINGS AND BEYOND WEED BEDS AS WELL AS THE WEED-FREE CHANNELS. USE ABOUT 2 FT. OF MONOFILAMENT LEADER BETWEEN HOOK AND SWIVEL. WITH DIPSEY ON LINE ABOVE SWIVEL IT WON'T SLIDE DOWN AGAINST CRAWFISH IN CASTING. ON THE BOTTOM, CRAWFISH CRAWLS UNCHECKED, PULLING OUT LINE BEHIND.

TEST LINE OFTEN TO PREVENT BAIT HIDING. LET FISH MOUTH BAIT A BIT BEFORE STRIKING.

203

HELLGRAMMITES ARE GOOD FISH BAIT

PASS HOOK UNDER COLLAR (AS SHALLOW AS POSSIBLE).

THE LARVA OF THE DOBSON FLY IS THE HELLGRAMMITE OR DOBSON CRAWLER. IT'S ALSO KNOWN BY MANY OTHER NAMES. DARK GRAYISH BROWN IN COLOR, ITS FLAT BODY IS SUITED FOR CRAWLING UNDER FLAT STONES IN A STREAM BED.

WADE QUIETLY INTO SHALLOW WATER AND TURN THE STONES OVER. IF CRAWLERS ARE PRESENT, THEY WILL MOVE OR BE MOVED BY THE CURRENT.

BE CAREFUL OF ITS PINCHERS Ⓐ IN HANDLING. A 3-INCHER CAN REALLY PINCH. IF YOU ARE NERVOUS ABOUT SUCH, CARRY TWEEZERS TO HOLD CRAWLER WHILE HOOKING IT.

204

BAIT FISHING WITH HELLGRAMMITES

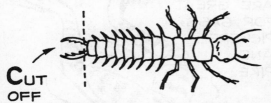

Cut OFF
TAIL PINCERS ALONG DOTTED
LINE BUT BE CAREFUL NOT
TO CUT INTO THE BODY.
WITHOUT THESE CLAWS THE
HELLGRAMMITE WILL NOT BE
ABLE TO HOLD ONTO A ROCK'S
BOTTOM AS SECURELY AS IT
WOULD WITH THEM. THUS IT'S
EASIER TO KEEP THEM VISIBLE
TO FISH AND YOU WON'T LOSE
SO MANY SNAGGED BY ROCKS.

WRAP — THREAD

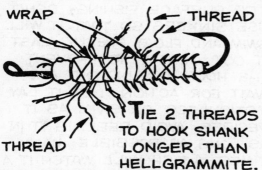

THREAD

Tie 2 THREADS
TO HOOK SHANK
LONGER THAN
HELLGRAMMITE.
WRAP AND TIE HIM AS ABOVE.
BAIT LIVES LONGER THUS.

205

BAITING WITH FROGS

SMALL FROGS
ARE GREAT
FOR BASS,
PICKEREL
AND
PIKE.

HOOK IT
THROUGH
BOTH LIPS
WITH THE
HOOK BARB
ON TOP AS
SHOWN SO
THE FROG WON'T DROWN.

FOR SURFACE FISHING, DON'T
USE SINKERS SO THAT IT WILL
SWIM AND FLOAT FREELY. CAST
IT OUT GENTLY TO PREVENT
THE HOOK TEARING OUT AND
WAIT FOR ACTION. LET IT LAY
MOTIONLESS OR SWIM AS IT
DECIDES. AVOID REELING IT IN
AS LONG AS POSSIBLE. MANY
TIMES, A FISH WILL WATCH IT A
LONG TIME BEFORE STRIKING.

SMALL FROGS ARE CHOICEST!

206

FROG HOOKING RIG

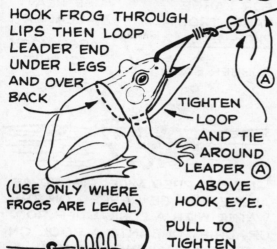

HOOK FROG THROUGH
LIPS THEN LOOP
LEADER END
UNDER LEGS
AND OVER
BACK

(USE ONLY WHERE
FROGS ARE LEGAL)

TIGHTEN
LOOP
AND TIE
AROUND
LEADER Ⓐ
ABOVE
HOOK EYE.

PULL TO
TIGHTEN

ALLOW EXTRA LEADER
AFTER TYING ON HOOK — TO
MAKE LOOP BACK AROUND FROG.

FIRST TIE HOOK ONTO THE
LEADER WITH THE KNOT SHOWN
JUST ABOVE. SEVERAL HOOKS
MAY BE TIED BEFOREHAND
FOR LESS BOTHER IN USING.
DON'T TRIM OR SKIMP ON THE
LEADER END WHEN TYING ON
THE HOOK SO A LOOP CAN BE
MADE. IT IS THE SNUG LOOP
AROUND THE FROG THAT PRE-
VENTS IT FLYING OFF THE
HOOK WHEN IT IS CAST.

207

FISHING A MOUSE...

FOR LARGE BASS, TROUT, PIKE, ETC.

USE HEAVY LEADER

LARGE HOOK TO SUIT

RUBBER BAND

LIVE-TRAPPED MICE, RIGGED AS ABOVE, MAY BE DAPPED ON THE WATER WITH A LONG, STIFF ROD. OR, DRIFT ONE INTO A POOL ON A BOARD, YANKING IT OFF IN A GOOD SPOT.

A STOUT LINE WITH A SLIDING RING ON IT CAN BE STRETCHED ABOVE A POOL WHERE A WISE OLD 'LUNKER' HIDES. ANOTHER SMALL RING SLIDES ON FISHING LEADER, ABOVE MOUSE. A BIT OF THREAD THAT BREAKS WHEN YOU SET HOOK IN FISH HOLDS RINGS

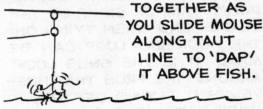

TOGETHER AS YOU SLIDE MOUSE ALONG TAUT LINE TO 'DAP' IT ABOVE FISH.

208

HOW TO PREPARE PORK RIND AS BAIT

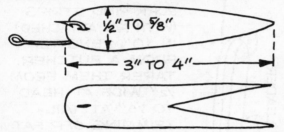

½" TO ⅝"

3" TO 4"

THIN PATTERNS TO TRY. THESE ARE GOOD SIZES FOR BASS, PIKE, PICKEREL AND WALLEYES. PAN FISH SIZES ARE SMALLER. CUT SHAPE WITH SCISSORS, EYELET FOR HOOK WITH A KNIFE POINT.

1¼"

1¾"

USE THICK RIND TO MAKE CHUNKS. CUT WITH A SHARP KNIFE.

SCRAPE RIND FREE OF ALL MEAT DOWN TO THE PORES. CUT PIECES INTO VARIOUS FROG OR MINNOW SHAPES OR AS ABOVE. FILL CLEAN, SMALL, AIR-TIGHT GLASS JAR WITH PIECES. POUR A SOLUTION OF 10% FORMALDEHYDE AND 90% WATER. SCREW LID TIGHT.

209

LONG PORK RINDS

GET EXTRA–TOUGH PORK RIND STRIPS (WITH FAT ATTACHED) IN 10" LENGTHS FROM A BUTCHER. TAPER THEM FROM ½" WIDE AT HEAD TO ⅛" AT TAIL, TRIMMING OFF FAT TO TAPER UNDERSIDE. PUNCH HOLE AT HEAD WITH ICE PICK FOR A 5/0 HOOK. PUNCH TWO HOLES, ½" APART, IN MIDDLE.

PRESERVE AND TOUGHEN STRIPS BY SOAKING IN A SOLUTION OF SALT AND WATER IN EQUAL PARTS.

TIE 5/0 HOOK TO MIDDLE WITH NYLON LEADER. INSERT HEAD HOOK.

TROLLED OR RETRIEVED, ITS WIGGLE LURES BASS, PIKE, ETC.

USE A SWIVEL IF LINE TWISTS.

20 LB. TEST LEADER (TIE TIGHT)

TOUGH RIND ON TOP

SILVER SPOON AND PORK RIND STRIPS

HERE IS ONE OF THE MOST POP-ULAR BAIT CASTING COMBINA-TION LURES.

THE PORK RIND FLUTTERS ENTICINGLY BE-HIND THE FLASH-ING SPOON. USED WITHOUT AN EXTRA TANDEM HOOK Ⓐ, IT IS PRACTICALLY WEEDLESS AND IS IDEAL FOR LARGE MOUTH BASS, ETC., WHICH MAY BE FEEDING IN SUCH SPOTS.

FOR SHORT STRIKING FISH RUN A SMALLER HOOK Ⓐ THROUGH THE STRIP'S END. IF THE RIND IS FRESH AND PROPERLY CURED, THE HOOK WILL HOLD BY ITS EYE Ⓑ.

KEEP ITS HOOK SHARP AND STRIKE QUICKLY WHEN A FISH HITS IT!

211

CATFISH BAITS...

Cut white laundry soap into small cubes. One cube on a hook gives off a soapy trail for distant catfish to follow to take your hook. They like soap! Spoil-free, it's cheap and <u>TURTLES</u> won't bother it!

Sponge bait is another popular lure. Cut sponge into small cubes and put them in a glass fruit jar. Cover cubes with meat scraps and dead minnows or fish. Limburger cheese and/or any entrails may be added. Cover and let 'ripen' for a week. Sponge absorbs odors and oil the 'cats' like. It washes out so change bait often.

212

KNOTS
YOU SHOULD KNOW

Practice tying these knots until you know them well. Otherwise you may make up a knot that by accident will pull out when a fish is on the line.

Don't trim the end of a knot too close or it will slip and come untied. Make certain that all knots are tight before using them. Then, after hooking and landing a fish, inspect the knot to see if it is still tight.

Most experienced anglers prefer to buy their hooks by the box and tie them directly onto the leader-end or tippet instead of using those already snelled on a card. Not only are they cheaper, but more important, there are fewer connections to warn the fish.

If a fish is undersized, merely cut the leader, leaving the hook in the fish to be dissolved after you release the fish. Then tie on a new 2-cent hook.

FLY-LINE SPLICE

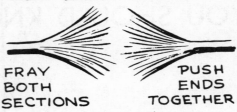

FRAY
BOTH
SECTIONS

PUSH
ENDS
TOGETHER

TWIST ENDS DOWN WITH A
BIT OF ROD VARNISH

WIND FROM THE MIDDLE OF
SPLICE OUTWARD WITH
SILK THREAD

HOLD →

FINISH SPLICE
WITH THIS KNOT → AND
PULL TIGHT. WIND LOOSE

END Ⓐ AND TIE YOUR
FINISH KNOT. TRIM AND
COAT WITH ROD VARNISH.

THIS STRONG SPLICE SLIPS
THROUGH THE GUIDES EASILY.

214

FLY LINE EYE-SPLICE IS EASY TO MAKE....

SCRAPE THE FINISH FROM
THE LINE'S END FOR ABOUT
3/8" AND FRAY THE THREADS
APART WITH A PIN. FIT A LOOP
AND SCRAPE LINE FINISH AT
THE JOINING.

RUB BEES-WAX
ON BOTH SECTIONS AND PRESS
THEM TOGETHER.

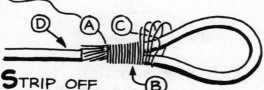

STRIP OFF
ABOUT 2 FT. OF SIZE OO
WINDING SILK THREAD AND
HOLDING AT Ⓐ, CAREFULLY
WIND CLOSELY WITHOUT OVER-
LAPPING TO BEYOND Ⓑ. FIN-
ISH BY PULLING TIGHT THE
INVISIBLE KNOT Ⓒ. REPEAT
WITH Ⓐ TO TIE AT Ⓓ. ROLL
IT SMOOTH. APPLY ROD VAR-
NISH. WHEN DRY, APPLY THE
SECOND COAT.

LEARN A GOOD KNOT

START A LEADER END
KNOT AS ABOVE--

TIGHTEN BY PULLING AT
"A" AND "B". TRIM "C".

BELOW IS ANOTHER
VERSION OF THE KNOT
ABOVE. THIS KNOT IS
THE STRONGER.

A DANDY FOR DROPPER
LEADER KNOTS ALSO!

216

LEARN A GOOD KNOT

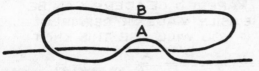

FOR A DROPPER LOOP--

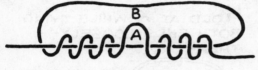

MAKE 4 ROLLS WITH "A"--

PULL "B" THROUGH "A"--
HOLD "B" AND TIGHTEN

SLOWLY BY PULLING "C's".

USEFUL ON EITHER LINE
OR NYLON LEADERS FOR
ADDING EXTRA HOOKS IN
BAIT OR FLY FISHING.

217

FISHING KNOTS

TAPERED LEADERS CAN BE EASILY MADE OR REPAIRED IF YOU WILL USE THIS KNOT

HOLD AT "X" WHILE TYING BOTH ENDS LOOSELY-- THEN--

PULL ENDS UP SNUG, ONE AT A TIME, NEXT--

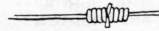

TIGHTEN SLOWLY AND TRIM ENDS

THIS **BARREL KNOT** IS THE STRONGEST KNOT FOR JOINING MONOFILA- MENT NYLON. USE STRANDS OF 1½, 2, 2½ AND 3 LBS. TEST IN EQUAL LENGTHS OR VARY TO SUIT YOUR NEEDS FOR A FINISHED TOTAL OF 8 TO 10 FT. LONG.

218

KNOTS FOR TYING LINE TO LEADER

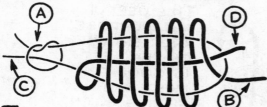

THIS KNOT PASSES SMOOTHLY THROUGH BAIT-CASTING ROD GUIDES IN CASTS OR RETRIEVES AND WEARS WELL. FORM A LOOP AT LEADER'S END, TYING TIGHT WITH SLIP KNOT (A). TIE A MULTIPLE CLINCH ABOUT THE LOOP WITH BAIT-CASTING LINE (B). PULL IT TIGHT SLOWLY, HOLDING LOOP AT (A). THEN PULL LEADER (C) TO JAM LOOP INTO LINE KNOT. TRIM ENDS (A) AND (D). IT'S NEAT!

TUCKED SHEET BEND KNOT IS USED TO TIE FLY LINE TO A NON-SLIP LEADER END LOOP. AVOID END (A) SLIPPING OUT OF LOOP WHILE TIGHTENING SLOWLY.

FISH HOOK KNOTS
-THE WOOD KNOT-

THIS USEFUL
ALL PURPOSE
KNOT SHOWN
ON THE LEFT
IS GOOD FOR
MOST BAIT
FISHING. WHEN
HOOK IS SNAGGED,
THE KNOT BREAKS,
THEREBY
SAVING THE
LEADER.

THE STRONGEST
AND VERY BEST
ALL-PURPOSE
KNOT IS
SHOWN AT
THE RIGHT.
THE BREAKING
POINT OF ANY
KNOT IS LESS
THAN THAT OF A
STRAIGHT KNOTLESS
STRAND. THIS KNOT
IS THE STRONGEST OF
ALL HOOK KNOTS!
MAKES A NEAT KNOT FOR
"THREADING" A WORM PAST
HOOK EYE FOR WARY FISH.

220

RUNNING KNOT

TIGHTEN Ⓐ PASS Ⓑ
OVER FLY AND PULL Ⓒ
TIGHT. THIS IS A DANDY
FLY KNOT!

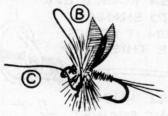

HOOK LEADER KNOT
SHOWN BELOW IS EASY
TO TIE -- IS GOOD FOR
BAIT CASTING.

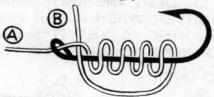

TRIM

PULL TIGHT AT Ⓐ AND Ⓑ

221

DOUBLE JAM KNOT

HOOK SHANK

PULL HERE
AND SLIP LOOP
OVER HOOK'S EYE
ONTO SHANK.
THEN IT LOOKS
LIKE THIS. →

PULL KNOT
TIGHT AGAINST
HOOK EYE.   ← TRIM

THIS KNOT IS
IDEAL FOR TYING FLIES ONTO
A LEADER. THE KNOT JAMS
TIGHTER WHEN A FISH PULLS
AGAINST IT. YET IT'S EASY
TO UNTIE TO CHANGE A FLY.

TO UNTIE,
PUSH
LINE
BACK
THROUGH EYE
AND PULL IT
DOWN.

222

GOOD NYLON KNOTS

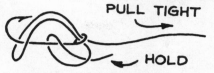

PULL TIGHT

HOLD

HOOK JAM KNOT

OTHER HOOK KNOTS MAY BE
EASIER TO TIE BUT FEW ARE
STRONGER. IT UNTIES EASILY.
USE FOR FLY OR BAIT HOOKS.

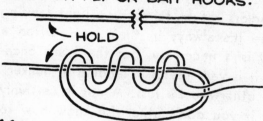

HOLD

HERE IS A KNOT TO JOIN TWO
STRANDS FOR A LEADER. LAY
ENDS PARALLEL. HOLD ONE END
WHILE TYING WITH BOTH STRANDS
AT ONCE AS SHOWN. TIGHTEN
SLOWLY, HOLDING BOTH STRANDS.

LOOP

TRIM

TIGHTEN

LEADER-END LOOP CAN BE
TIED WITH 2 SLIP KNOTS. JAM
TIGHTENED KNOTS TOGETHER.

223

HANDY EQUIPMENT

You can always find handy extra items for fishing but you must consider their weight and how much equipment will be comfortable to carry.

Some anglers refuse to carry a light landing net because it's always in their way. Often a landing net isn't necessary, but there are occasions when it is very useful in landing a "lunker" that might otherwise be lost. A net is certainly a big help if you don't otherwise know how to land your fish! Always submerge the net and lead the fish over it before lifting him head first into the net.

Besides the net, you'll need a knife, a small sharpening stone for hooks and knife, small pliers that can close a sinker or cut a fish hook in tow, Mercurochrome, Band-aids, a creel or stringer and a bait-carrier (if bait fishing). A plug caster needs a tackle box with shelved compartments. The fly caster should have a fly hook or box. All can use a convenient leader dispenser. These are basic, and you can add more as you need.

TACKLE BOX TIPS

THE HOT
SUN RAYS ON
EXPOSED TACKLE BOXES
WILL HEAT THE INSIDES
LIKE AN OVEN. THIS HEAT
DAMAGES LURES, ETC., SO
SHADE THE BOX IF POSSIBLE.

ALUMINUM FINISHED BOXES
REFLECT THE SUN RAYS SO
LESS HEAT IS ABSORBED
TO PASS INSIDE.   DARK
FINISHED METAL BOXES
 DO   NOT   REFLECT AND
    ARE HOTTEST INSIDE.

PAINT YOUR BOX WITH
WHITE ENAMEL TO REFLECT
THE SUN AND PREVENT
RUST OR CORROSION!

NEAT HOOK PACKS

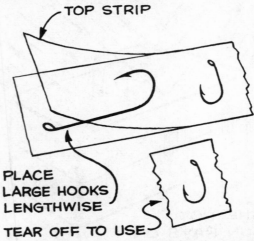

TOP STRIP

PLACE
LARGE HOOKS
LENGTHWISE

TEAR OFF TO USE

LAY LOOSE HOOKS ON THE
STICKY SIDE OF CELLOPHANE
TAPE, 1" WIDE. COVER WITH A
SECOND STRIP, STICKY SIDE DOWN.
USE A DIFFERENT STRIP FOR
EACH SIZE HOOK. HOOKS RE-
MAIN SHARP WITHOUT TANGLING.

SOME OF
THE LARGER
STRAIGHT-EYED
HOOKS CAN BE
STRUNG ON A
SAFETY PIN TO
KEEP IN A CON-
TAINER OR YOUR TACKLE BOX.

226

GANG HOOK GUARD PROTECTS FINGERS

SLIDE CORK DOWN THE HOOK SHANK PRESSING POINTS INTO THE CORK.

SLIP CORK ONTO HOOK SHANK.

SLICE A BOTTLE CORK INTO THREE PIECES AND MAKE A CUT HALF-WAY THROUGH EACH PIECE.

WHEN BAIT CASTING PLUGS ARE NOT KEPT IN INDIVIDUAL COMPARTMENTS OF A TACKLE BOX TRAY THEY BECOME A NUISANCE WHEN TOSSED LOOSELY IN THE BOTTOM OF THE BOX. THIS CORK ALSO PROTECTS THE PLUGS' FINISH FROM THE HOOK BARBS.

NYLON FISHING LINES WON'T ROT!

Nylon line will usually outwear linen or silk because it is not necessary to rinse it in fresh water and dry it before it is put away after using each time. Neglect other lines and they will rot; and undiscovered, this may cause the loss of a prize fish!

So long, Bub!

TRANSFERRING LINE FROM SPOOL TO REEL

Do NOT REEL A NEW LINE FROM A SPOOL THAT LIES

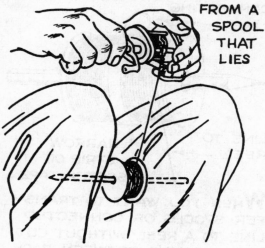

FLAT ON ITS SIDE. TO DO SO CAUSES A TWIST FOR EVERY TURN OF THE SPOOL.

To PREVENT LINE TWIST, PUSH A PENCIL THROUGH THE SPOOL'S CENTER AND HAVE SOMEONE HOLD IT AS YOU WIND IT ONTO THE REEL.

You CAN DO IT YOURSELF BY PLACING THE PENCIL ENDS IN BACK OF YOUR BENT KNEES AND REELING AS ABOVE.

229

TRANSFERRING A CONNECTED LINE TO A REEL.........

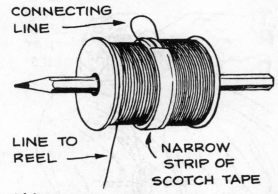

CONNECTING
LINE →

LINE TO
REEL →

NARROW
STRIP OF
SCOTCH TAPE

WHEN YOU WANT TO TRANS-
FER SPOOLS OF CONNECTED
LINE TO A REEL WITHOUT CUT-
TING THE LINE BETWEEN EACH
SPOOL TRY THIS.

PLACE THE SPOOLS SIDE BY
SIDE AND SECURE THEM TO-
GETHER WITH NARROW STRIPS
OF SCOTCH TAPE ALONG THEIR
RIMS. RUN A PENCIL THROUGH
SPOOLS AS SHOWN. ALL SPOOLS
TURN TOGETHER. WHEN ONE IS
REELED EMPTY, USE FINGERS
CAREFULLY TO PICK OUT LOOPS
OF NEXT SPOOL'S START. THUS,
THE FILLED REEL IS KNOTLESS.

RETRIEVER SAVES SNAGGED PLUGS

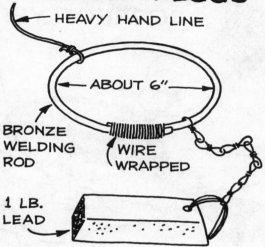

HEAVY HAND LINE

ABOUT 6"

BRONZE WELDING ROD

WIRE WRAPPED

1 LB. LEAD

SHAPE A BRONZE ROD INTO A CIRCLE AND SLIP THE END OF A SMALL, 6 IN. CHAIN ONTO IT. WIRE-WRAP THE OVERLAPPING CIRCLE ENDS. PUNCH A HOLE THROUGH A 1 LB. BLOCK OF LEAD TO WIRE IT TO THE CHAIN. TIE ENOUGH HEAVY LINE ONTO THE RING TO REACH DOWN TO SNAGGED LURE. LINE MAY BE REELED ON EXTRA REEL OR COILED.

WHEN PLUG SNAGS, SLIDE RING OVER ROD, REEL AND DOWN LINE. JIGGLE WITH HAND LINE TO FREE.

231

DO YOU USE A LANDING NET CORRECTLY?

ALWAYS TIRE
THE FISH COMPLETELY
BEFORE USING THE NET.
OTHERWISE THE FISH MIGHT
FIGHT THE NET AND ESCAPE.
DO NOT SWIPE AT THE FISH
WITH THE NET. DIP THE NET
FIRST SO THAT NETTING
DOES NOT FLOAT, LEAVE
NET FRAME ALMOST SUBMER-
GED AT AN ANGLE. LEAD FISH
<u>OVER</u> NET THEN RAISE NET.

232

FISH NETTING TIP...

CURRENT →

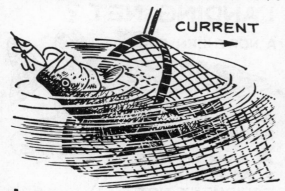

LEAD PLUG-HOOKED FISH INTO THE CURRENT ON A TAUT LINE. THEN LET THEM DROP DOWN-STREAM INTO THE SUBMERGED NET, TAIL FIRST, AS SHOWN. IN CALM WATERS, HOLD A FISH'S HEAD ABOVE THE SURFACE AND RAISE THE SUBMERGED NET A-BOUT THE FISH. THUS, A FISH CAN'T SNAG THE LURE IN NET'S TOP UPON ENTERING AND POSSIBLY ES-CAPE. WHEN FISH IS NETTED, LIFT AND TURN NET'S TOP SIDE-WISE TO CLOSE IT.

MANY ANGLERS PREFER TO NET __ALL__ FISH THUS IN-STEAD OF HEAD FIRST.

233

GAFF HOOK OR .....
LANDING NET ?

A NORTHERN PIKE

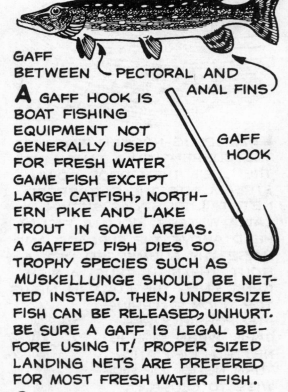

GAFF
BETWEEN ⌐ PECTORAL AND
ANAL FINS

GAFF
HOOK

A GAFF HOOK IS
BOAT FISHING
EQUIPMENT NOT
GENERALLY USED
FOR FRESH WATER
GAME FISH EXCEPT
LARGE CATFISH, NORTH-
ERN PIKE AND LAKE
TROUT IN SOME AREAS.
A GAFFED FISH DIES SO
TROPHY SPECIES SUCH AS
MUSKELLUNGE SHOULD BE NET-
TED INSTEAD. THEN, UNDERSIZE
FISH CAN BE RELEASED, UNHURT.
BE SURE A GAFF IS LEGAL BE-
FORE USING IT! PROPER SIZED
LANDING NETS ARE PREFERED
FOR MOST FRESH WATER FISH.

GAFFS ARE USED MOSTLY FOR
BOATING LARGE SALT WATER FISH.

GAFF A BEATEN FISH IN ONE
CAREFUL UP-SWEEPING ACTION.

HOOK DISGORGER DOES A NEAT JOB!

WALLEYES, PICKEREL, NORTHERN PIKE AND MUSKIES HAVE SHARP TEETH AND SOMETIMES IT'S A CHORE TO REMOVE A HOOK WITHOUT FIRST KILLING THEM. PUT FISH ON STRINGER BEFORE TAKING IT FROM THE NET. THEN PARALYZE IT WHILE USING THE DISGORGER BY PRESSURE ON THE EYE SOCKETS. STRINGERED AND BACK IN THE WATER, FISH REMAIN FRESH LONGER. SHOWING ONE TYPE OF DISGORGER IN USE.

235

SEE UNDERWATER WITH THIS TUBE...

IT'S EASY TO LOCATE UNDER-WATER SPRINGS, WEEDS, ETC. WHERE FISH SCHOOL-UP IN A LAKE FOR ITS BEST FISHING.

MAKE A ROLL OF TARPAPER AND SECURE ITS OVERLAPPING EDGES WITH NARROW STRIPS OF WOOD OR LATH, INSIDE AND OUT-SIDE, NAILED TOGETHER. STRING WILL HOLD SHAPED ROLL WHILE SLIPPING ROLL ONTO A SUSPENDED TIMBER TO NAIL.

AVOID MOSQUITOES

TAPE OR TIE WITH CORD →

← POLE OR OAR

"STILL FISHING" AT NIGHT SOME-TIMES PRODUCES THE BEST FISHING AND MOST MOSQUITO-ES. AVOID THE PESTS BY HANGING A LANTERN FROM A POLE SECURED IN THE BOAT. THE LIGHT ATTRACTS THE BUGS AND LEAVES YOU FREE TO ENJOY THE FISHING. CHECK LOCAL NIGHT FISHING LAWS.

WADING STAFF IS A STREAM HELPER

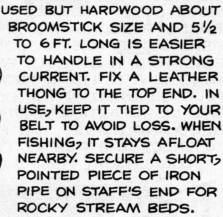

A WADING STAFF AIDS GREATLY IN FEELING OUT DEEP HOLES IN A QUIET STREAM OR AS A PROP FOR STABILITY IN CROSSING A SWIFT STREAM. BAMBOO MAY BE USED BUT HARDWOOD ABOUT BROOMSTICK SIZE AND 5½ TO 6 FT. LONG IS EASIER TO HANDLE IN A STRONG CURRENT. FIX A LEATHER THONG TO THE TOP END. IN USE, KEEP IT TIED TO YOUR BELT TO AVOID LOSS. WHEN FISHING, IT STAYS AFLOAT NEARBY. SECURE A SHORT, POINTED PIECE OF IRON PIPE ON STAFF'S END FOR ROCKY STREAM BEDS.

DISJOINT FLY ROD WITH LINE ON FOR RISKY CROSSINGS.

238

WARMER WEATHER WADING . . . .

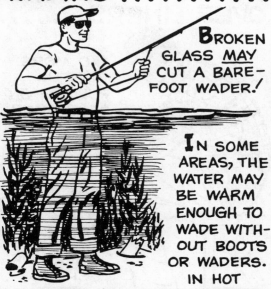

BROKEN GLASS <u>MAY</u> CUT A BARE-FOOT WADER.!

IN SOME AREAS, THE WATER MAY BE WARM ENOUGH TO WADE WITH-OUT BOOTS OR WADERS. IN HOT WEATHER, WADERS CAN BECOME UNCOMFORTABLE AND DAMP IN-SIDE FROM PERSPIRATION AND WATER CONDENSATION. AT SUCH TIMES IT MAY BE MORE COMFORT-ABLE TO WEAR OLD TROUSERS AND A PAIR OF RUBBER-SOLED CANVAS SHOES IF IT'S A LEVEL BOTTOM. HEAVIER WADING SHOES SHOULD BE WORN WHERE IT IS ROUGH OR BOULDER STREWN.

CHANGE OR DRY CLOTHING AS SOON AS POSSIBLE AFTERWARD.!

HOW TO PUT RUBBER BOOTS ON EASILY OVER LINERS.......

No MORE PAINFUL PULLING ON OF RUBBER BOOTS OVER SHEEPSKIN OR FELT

LINERS OR SHOES!

Place ENOUGH STRIPS OF SCOTCH TAPE AROUND THE HEEL OF THE LINER AND YOUR FOOT WILL SLIP MORE EASILY INTO RUBBER BOOTS!

240

CORRECT STORAGE FOR WADERS......

WRONG

WHEN STORING WADERS FOR THE SEASON, <u>DON'T HANG THEM IN ANY MANNER</u>!

MANY SPORTSMEN WRONGLY BELIEVE THAT WADERS SHOULD BE HUNG SO AIR WILL CIRCULATE THROUGH THEM. PERHAPS THEY DON'T KNOW THAT AIR AND LIGHT CAUSE RUBBER TO DETERIORATE!

ALL FINE RUBBER, <u>INCLUDING WADERS</u>, SHOULD BE CLEANED WITH SOAP AND WATER AND <u>RINSED</u> COMPLETELY THEN ROLLED CAREFULLY AND WRAPPED TIGHT IN HEAVY PAPER, FORCING AIR OUT IN WRAPPING. ADD A CELLOPHANE WRAP AND STORE IN A COOL PLACE.

241

HOW TO KEEP FISH

The average keeper-sized fish released by the fish hatcheries may cost the State one dollar or more. So, if you don't intend to use your catch for food or a trophy, release it instead of letting it die for nothing.

All fish taste better if they are killed, cleaned and iced or wrapped in dampened leaves or grass, and placed in a creel soon after the catch is made. Remember in cleaning to remove the gills and with your thumbnail remove the kidney which lies along the spine. Then wipe the insides clean.

Splash water occasionally over the grass-covered fish to prevent drying out. If fish do dry out, soak them in cold water before cooking. Drying out may ruin the best flavor and texture, but some anglers don't think so. Dried fish will keep longer without refrigeration.

When fishing in a boat, in preference to stringers, try cracked ice in a wash tub fitted with a draincock and covered with damp burlap to keep fish until you come in. A variation is to mix sawdust with the ice and wrap each fish in wax paper before burrowing it deep. Small portable refrigerators are excellent also — just keep the fish out of the ice water in the bottom.

HOW TO RELEASE
UNDERSIZED FISH...

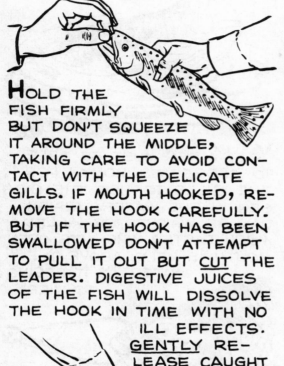

Hold the
FISH FIRMLY
BUT DON'T SQUEEZE
IT AROUND THE MIDDLE,
TAKING CARE TO AVOID CON-
TACT WITH THE DELICATE
GILLS. IF MOUTH HOOKED, RE-
MOVE THE HOOK CAREFULLY.
BUT IF THE HOOK HAS BEEN
SWALLOWED DON'T ATTEMPT
TO PULL IT OUT BUT <u>CUT</u> THE
LEADER. DIGESTIVE JUICES
OF THE FISH WILL DISSOLVE
THE HOOK IN TIME WITH NO
ILL EFFECTS.
<u>GENTLY</u> RE-
LEASE CAUGHT
FISH IN A
QUIET POOL
TO RECOVER.

243

CAN FISH DROWN?

YES! A FISH MUST BE ABLE TO CLOSE ITS MOUTH FOR THE GILLS TO USE THE OXYGEN IN THE WATER. A FISH CAN BE WHIPPED OR KILLED MUCH FASTER WHEN ITS OPEN MOUTH IS HELD ABOVE THE WATER AS IT BEGINS TO TIRE.

FOR THIS REASON HOOK THE FISH THROUGH BOTH THE UPPER AND LOWER LIPS WHEN PUTTING IT ON A STRINGER, IF YOU WANT IT KEPT ALIVE.

244

STRINGERED FISH AND THE BOAT.....

SUN

WRONG   RIGHT

KEEP LIVE FISH
IN THE SHADE
OF THE BOAT
AS MUCH AS
POSSIBLE AND
LENGTHEN THE STRINGER
SO THE FISH CAN GO DOWN
TO COOLER WATER. IN THE SUN
AND NEAR THE SURFACE, FISH
PERISH QUICKLY.

LEAVE FISH IN THE WATER BE-
HIND A BOAT WHEN TROLLING
SLOWLY BUT TAKE ABOARD WHEN
MOVING FAST OR THEY'LL DROWN.

245

CARRY YOUR FISH IN A WILLOW CREEL!

NOTHING KEEPS FISH COOL AND FRESH AS WELL AS THE WHOLE WILLOW CREEL.

REMOVE GILLS AND INNARDS AND WIPE INSIDES OF FISH CLEAN AS THEY ARE CAUGHT. WRAP EACH LOOSELY WITH FERN, LEAVES OR GRASS AND PLACE ON TWIGS IN CREEL. IT'S IMPORTANT THAT FISH DO NOT TOUCH CREEL OR OTHER FISH. SPLASH WATER OVER ALL AT REGULAR INTERVALS. AIR CIR-CULATION REFRIGERATES YOUR PRIZES.

KEEP FISH WITHOUT REFRIGERATION.....

HEAD OFF

SLIT BELLY

Remove any red trace of gills remaining after cutting off the head. Remove entrails and the dark strip along the backbone. Use <u>no</u> water but dry wipe fish clean!

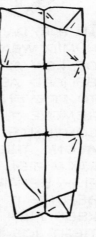

Tightly wrap each fish separately. First in wax paper then newspaper and tie it with string. So wrapped and kept in the shade, fish will keep 3 or 4 days but fish must be cleaned without delay!

247

HOW TO KEEP KILLED FISH FOR LATER USE

IN HOT DAMP HUMID WEATHER OF LOW AREAS, FISH SHOULD BE ICED AS SOON AS POSSIBLE TO PREVENT SPOILAGE. REMOVE THE GILLS, STOMACH CONTENTS AND KIDNEY (LYING ALONG THE SPINE) AND WIPE EACH FISH DRY. WRAP EACH FISH SEPARATELY IN PAPER BEFORE IT IS ICED. DO NOT KEEP FISH TOO LONG IN AIR TIGHT ICE BOXES FOR STALE AIR TAINTS FISH. CLEAN BOX WITH BOILING SODA-WATER.

248

KEEPING TROUT IN A HIGH, DRY ALTITUDE

Remove fish innards and wipe dry each when caught. Wrap each in brown paper before placing it in your creel. In camp, unwrap and salt and pepper the trout's insides. Hang, as above, on a wire between two trees in the <u>shade</u>. Don't crowd them together! Keep them outside at night and out of the sun during the day. Protect them from rain also.

Like "jerky" when dry, soak for 30 min. before cooking.

249

KEEPING FISH FOR THE TAXIDERMIST

NOT ALL ANGLERS ARE SKILLED IN SKINNING A TROPHY FISH SO THIS IS HOW TO PRESERVE IT FOR THE TAXIDERMIST TO SKIN.

KILL FISH IMMEDIATELY WITH A SMART BLOW ON TOP OF ITS HEAD WITH A "BILLY" OR KNIFE HANDLE BUT <u>DON'T</u> <u>BRUISE</u>! WRAP IT IN <u>WET</u> BURLAP FIRST THEN IN CANVAS (AVOID NEWSPAPER, INK MAY DISCOLOR). HEAD FOR CAMP. ICE AND KEEP BURLAP WET SO THE FISH SCALES DON'T COME LOOSE! HURRY IT TO THE TAXIDERMIST!

PREPARING A FISH TROPHY FOR THE TAXIDERMIST........

MEASURE LENGTH AND GIRTH OF FISH AND TRACE ITS OUTLINE ON PAPER. MAKE COLOR NOTES AND WEIGH FISH.

MIX ALUM INTO WATER UNTIL NO MORE DISSOLVES TO WASH SLIME FROM FISH.

THE DOTTED LINE IN THE SKETCH OF THE MUSKY SHOWS HOW TO CUT FROM HEAD TO TAIL, OPPOSITE THE BEST-LOOKING SIDE OF THE FISH FOR REMOVING ITS INSIDES. CAREFULLY AVOID FURTHER CUTTING OF SKIN OR ITS WHITE LINING. RE-MOVE SKULL'S INSIDES, GILLS AND EYES. RINSE SKIN IN SALT WATER AND DRAIN IT. SALT BOTH SIDES AND STRAIGHTEN. RE-SALT IN 2 DAYS. SHIP FLAT.

251

COOKING
YOUR FISH

To round out your knowledge of fishing you will want to know something about cooking.

If you are married, you can impress your wife when she goes along by "pitching-in" to prepare your fish and cook it. Get her interested in angling to make it doubly enjoyable for both of you! You will then have an understanding fishing partner to share your joys afloat or along the stream.

FISH FLAVOR TIPS

PICKEREL

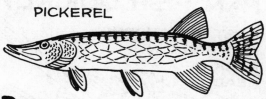

PART OF THE MUDDY FLAVOR OF SOME FISH SUCH AS PICKEREL, ROCK BASS, ETC. IS DUE TO THE WATER THEY LIVE IN. THE BEST FLAVORED OF THESE FISH ARE THOSE THAT INHABIT THE FRESHEST WATERS.

MUCH OF THE MUDDY FLAVOR CAN BE ELIMINATED AFTER THE FISH IS SCALED BY SCRAPING THE SLIME OFF WITH A KNIFE-BLADE AND RINSING SEVERAL TIMES UNTIL NO <u>BLACK</u> SLIME RESULTS. THIS APPLIES TO ANY FISH NOT NORMALLY SKINNED. SOME ANGLERS PREFER TO SKIN ALL MUD-FLAVORED FISH.

A TABLE FORK IS SUITABLE FOR A SCALER. WET FISH FIRST THEN SCALE FROM TAIL TO HEAD AS SHOWN.

253

HOW TO CLEAN PAN FISH QUICKLY

FIRST CUT THROUGH
BACKBONE IN
BACK OF
HEAD

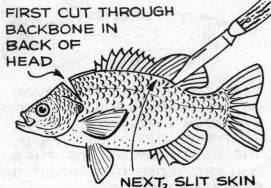

NEXT, SLIT SKIN
ON BOTH SIDES OF DORSAL FIN
FROM 1ST CUT TO TAIL. THEN
PEEL SKIN BACK IN A TRIANGLE
FROM BOTH CUTS.

NOW
BEND THE
HEAD DOWN WITH LEFT HAND,
PASSING RIGHT-HAND FINGERS
UNDER BACKBONE TO LIFT UP.
THE MEAT COMES OUT FREE OF
SKIN, HEAD AND ENTRAILS. PULL
OUT DORSAL FIN AND CUT OFF TAIL.

BONE-FREE FILLETS

SLIT THE FISH SKIN FROM HEAD TO TAIL ALONG THE BACK BESIDE THE DORSAL FIN Ⓑ. THEN SLIT DOWN THE SIDE FROM HEAD Ⓐ TO THE FRONT OF THE ANAL FIN Ⓒ. NEXT SLIT FROM Ⓒ ALONGSIDE THE ANAL FIN TO THE TAIL. LIFT ONLY THE SKIN AT Ⓔ AND PULL IT BACK TO THE TAIL WITH THE EDGE OF THE BLADE.

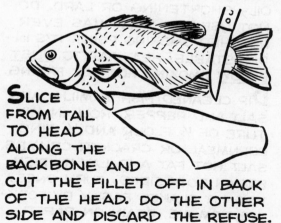

SLICE FROM TAIL TO HEAD ALONG THE BACKBONE AND CUT THE FILLET OFF IN BACK OF THE HEAD. DO THE OTHER SIDE AND DISCARD THE REFUSE.

255

TASTY FRIED FISH

MELT, IN A CAST IRON SKILLET (BEST FOR FRYING FISH), TO ½" DEEP, CLEAN, ODORLESS COOKING OIL, SHORTENING OR LARD. DO NOT USE FAT THAT HAS EVER REACHED SMOKING POINT. IT'S IN-DIGESTABLE! HEAT FAT TO JUST BELOW SMOKING HOT FOR FRYING.

DIP CLEANED FISH IN MILK, ADD SALT AND PEPPER, ROLL IN MIX-TURE OF ½ FLOUR AND ½ FINE CORNMEAL OR CRACKER CRUMBS. SALT HOT FAT AND LAY IN FISH. BROWN BOTH SIDES, TURN ONCE. WHEN IT FLAKES EASILY BY FORK-ING, REMOVE. DRAIN ON PAPER.

BROILED FISH IS A STREAMSIDE TREAT

WIRE BIG TROUT OR NON-FATTY FISH THAT ARE CLEANED, SALT AND PEPPERED, TO SPLIT HALVES OF A SHORT LOG. LEAN THESE AGAINST A FALLEN LOG OR ROCKS. BUILD FIRE CLOSE ENOUGH TO COOK BUT NOT BURN FISH. YOU CAN CONTINUE TO FISH WHILE IT COOKS. FISH ARE USUALLY DONE WHEN THE FIRE BURNS DOWN. IM-PALE OR WIRE SMALL FISH ONTO GREEN STICKS STUCK IN GROUND.

257

BARBECUED FISH

-LARGE TROUT, SALMON, BASS, ETC.-
BROWN FLESH
SIDE FIRST

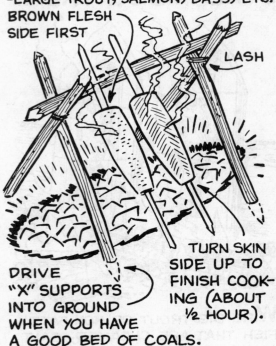

LASH

TURN SKIN
SIDE UP TO
FINISH COOK-
ING (ABOUT
½ HOUR).

DRIVE
"X" SUPPORTS
INTO GROUND
WHEN YOU HAVE
A GOOD BED OF COALS.

USE GREEN HARDWOOD SAP-
LINGS FOR "X" SUPPORTS 3 FT.
LONG AND CROSS PIECE (ITS
LENGTH DEPENDS ON NUMBER
OF FISH TO COOK). USE SMALL-
ER SAPLINGS FOR SKEWERS.
BUILD A DRY HARDWOOD FIRE IN
A PRE-DUG TRENCH. CLEAN, SCALE,
FILLET (SPLIT AND REMOVE BACK-
BONE) AND SEASON.

CLEANING CATFISH

HOLD THUMB IN MOUTH AND
CUT DORSAL FIN AS SHOWN--
IN LINE WITH GILLS.

LOOSEN SKIN ON BACK WITH
KNIFE EDGE (A). CUT SKIN (B)
FROM DORSAL FIN CUT TO TAIL.
CUT BACKBONE AND FLESH
BEHIND HEAD AT (C). NOW
HOLD HEAD AND
PRY BACK (D)

UP FROM HEAD. WITH A FIRM
GRIP AT (D) PULL EDIBLE PART
AWAY FROM THE REFUSE.

259

PREPARING A TURTLE

DON'T
THROW IT
BACK IN!

SNAPPING
TURTLE

TO PREPARE A TURTLE FOR
COOKING: CUT OFF THE HEAD
AND FEET. WITH ITS BACK TO
A BOARD, TIE OR NAIL THE TAIL
DOWN. CUT AWAY THE SKIN
AROUND THE LOWER EDGE OF
THE BACK SHELL. CUT LOOSE
THE BELLY PLATE. SKIN THE
NECK, TAIL AND QUARTERS BE-
FORE REMOVING THEM. THESE
ARE THE EDIBLES. IF IT'S A
LARGE ONE, REMOVE AND DIS-
CARD THE ORGANS THEN TAKE
OUT THE TASTY TENDERLOINS
NEXT TO THE BACK. REMOVE
FAT AND RINSE IN WATER.

TURTLE MEAT
IS VERY MUCH
LIKE CHICKEN!

FISHING IN SAFETY

Always look behind you before casting. Never side-cast a plug if it might endanger people nearby. Be careful of yourself when fly-casting by keeping the back-cast high. A fly hook carried by a flying line can make a dangerous wound.

Carry a small bottle of Mercurochrome to disinfect any scratch or wound. Carry pliers to remove a hook.

Beware of deep holes and slippery rocks when wading, especially in swift water. Learn how to wade a stream! Some anglers carry a light staff for a prop and to feel out the depths ahead when wading in fast water.

Don't overload a small boat with passengers when fishing. Two anglers may fish from one boat, and three may be a crowd — and unsafe! Extra passengers along for the ride usually crowd the serious fishermen. Don't stand in a boat when playing or netting a fish, if you can avoid it. Carry buoyant cushions aboard for each passenger as they will serve a double purpose, even though everyone aboard can swim.

Be careful when climbing over boulder-strewn banks to prevent a fall. Carry a small canteen or bottle of drinking water instead of chancing the local fishing water.

DO'S AND DON'TS IN USING BOATS...

DON'T FOLLOW COMMON PRACTICE AT MANY LAKE RESORTS OF RACING PAST ANGLERS IN YOUR MOTOR BOAT. THE WAKE DISTURBS THEM, EVEN FROM A DISTANCE.

DON'T OVERLOAD ANGLER-BOATS WITH SIGHTSEERS. ONLY 2 CAN FISH FROM MOST SMALL BOATS AT ONCE, OTHERS ARE IN THE WAY.

DO HEAD FOR LAND WHEN STORMS APPROACH. THEREFORE USE A MOTOR WITH SUFFICIENT POWER ON LARGE LAKES. IT'S QUICKER TO BEST FISHING SPOTS ALSO.

FISHING BOAT TIPS

DON'T STAND UP TO CAST OR PLAY A FISH FROM A ROWBOAT OR CANOE. IN THE EXCITEMENT YOU MAY GO OVERBOARD. REMEMBER THAT A STANDING PERSON IS MORE EASILY SEEN BY A FISH ALSO.

WITH TWO PEOPLE IN A BOAT IT'S EASIER FOR ONE TO NET HIS FISH WHILE HIS PARTNER HANDLES THE OARS. KEEP BOAT MOVING AWAY FROM APPROACHING HOOKED FISH TO PREVENT IT GOING UNDER THE BOAT.

DON'T BANG OARS, TACKLE BOXES, ETC. IN A BOAT; SOUND VIBRATES TO SCARE FISH AWAY.

BOAT PROTECTION FROM LIGHTNING!

COPPER WIRE ATTACHED TO KEEL STRIP AT BOTTOM

CLAMP A CANE POLE INSIDE BOW

ELECTRIC STORMS CAN BE DANGEROUS TO OCCUPANTS OF SMALL BOATS ON OPEN WATERS.

METAL STRIP SECURED TO BOAT'S KEEL

IT IS AUTHORITATIVELY CLAIMED THAT LIGHTNING STRIKE DANGER IS REDUCED TO ONE IN A THOUS- AND WITH THIS GROUNDING RIG.

RIG GROUNDS METAL HULLS ALSO.

264

BEACHING BOATS

BEACHING AN
ARKANSAS
JOHN
BOAT

SELECT AN AREA WITHOUT UN-
DERWATER SNAGS OR JAGGED
ROCKS AND A SMOOTH BEACH
TO PULL YOUR BOAT OR CANOE
UPON. PULL IT CLEAR OF THE
WATER AND POSSIBLE HIGH LEV-
ELS. OTHERWISE, WAVES KEEP
MOVING THE BOAT TO AND FRO,
GRINDING THE BOTTOM ON THE
SAND.

TIE THE PAINTER (ROPE IN BOW)
TO A BOULDER, BUSH OR TREE.
OR, CARRY THE ANCHOR BACK
ON THE BEACH AS FAR AS YOU
CAN. IF BOAT IS TOO HEAVY TO
HANDLE, ANCHOR IN WATER DEEP
ENOUGH TO FLOAT IT, NEAR SHORE.

BOAT ANCHORS

A REMOTE CONTROL ANCHOR IS HANDY IN BOAT FISHING.

THE ANGLER CAN OPERATE IT, MOTOR OR OARS AND FISH FROM ONE POSITION WITHOUT MOVING ABOUT IN THE BOAT TO ALARM THE FISH.

ONE ANCHOR AT EACH END OF A BOAT KEEPS IT FROM SWINGING AROUND...

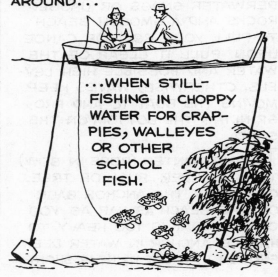

...WHEN STILL-FISHING IN CHOPPY WATER FOR CRAPPIES, WALLEYES OR OTHER SCHOOL FISH.

CANOE ACCIDENTS...

NON-SWIMMERS SHOULD STAY WITH A CANOE BUT NOT TRY FLOATING ON AN OVERTURNED ONE. ITS ROLLING ACTION IS HAZARDOUS!

INSTEAD, SWING THE CANOE RIGHTSIDE-UP AND CRAWL IN. EVEN THOUGH IT IS FULL OF WATER, YOU CAN FLOAT, FACE UP, WITH ELBOWS SUPPORTED ON TOP THE BOAT GUNWALES AND HANDS CLASPED BEHIND YOUR HEAD! <u>DON'T</u> <u>TRY</u> <u>TO</u> <u>SIT</u> <u>UP</u> <u>OR</u> <u>IT</u> <u>WON'T</u> <u>FLOAT</u> <u>YOU</u>! YOU CAN SPLASH WATER OUT WITH YOUR HANDS BUT IT IS TIRESOME IN THIS POSITION.

STANDARD ALUMINUM CANOE HAS BUILT-IN AIR CHAMBERS. IT RIGHTS ITSELF AND SUPPORTS EVEN IF FULL OF WATER!

267

SPLASHING WATER OUT OF A CANOE....

GUNWALE

FIRST TURN THE CANOE UPRIGHT.
THEN PUT YOUR WEIGHT AT ONE END
AND SHOVE CANOE BOW FORWARD.
MUCH OF THE WATER IS REMOVED
AFTER ANOTHER SHOVE. NOW
MOVE AROUND TO MID-CENTER
OF THE SIDE. GRASP GUNWALE
AND RAISE YOURSELF BY PUSHING
DOWN AND AWAY (AS SHOWN ABOVE)
THEN RELAX AND REPEAT. CONTIN-
UE AND SOON NEARLY ALL WATER
IS "ROCKED" OUT.

HOW TO CLIMB IN

REACH ACROSS AND GRASP FAR
SIDE GUNWALE. PULL YOURSELF
OVER PAST THE CANOE'S CENTER.
TWISTING, SIT DOWN. YOU'RE IN!

ADAPT OLD SHOES FOR SAFE WADING

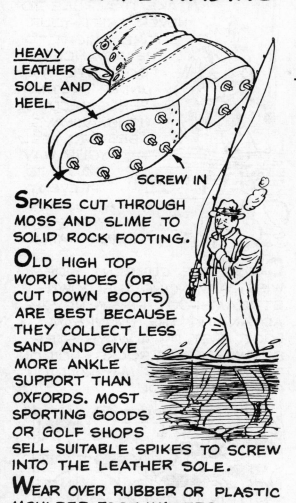

HEAVY
LEATHER
SOLE AND
HEEL

SCREW IN

SPIKES CUT THROUGH MOSS AND SLIME TO SOLID ROCK FOOTING.

OLD HIGH TOP WORK SHOES (OR CUT DOWN BOOTS) ARE BEST BECAUSE THEY COLLECT LESS SAND AND GIVE MORE ANKLE SUPPORT THAN OXFORDS. MOST SPORTING GOODS OR GOLF SHOPS SELL SUITABLE SPIKES TO SCREW INTO THE LEATHER SOLE.

WEAR OVER RUBBER OR PLASTIC MOULDED-FOOT WADERS.

269

WADING A STREAM

MAKE IT A RULE TO NEVER SHIFT YOUR ENTIRE WEIGHT TO THE ADVANCED FOOT UNTIL THE UNDER FOOTING FEELS SECURE. IT IS ALWAYS BEST TO FEEL YOUR WAY SO AS TO PREVENT A SUDDEN DROP-OFF INTO DEEPER WATER.

CURRENT

CROSS THE CURRENT SIDE-WISE, ADVANCING THE DOWN-STREAM-FOOT FIRST, NEVER ADVANCING THE UPSTREAM FOOT PAST IT. ALWAYS STEP BETWEEN THE ROCKS, NOT ON THEM FOR THEY MAY ROLL OUT FROM UNDER YOU.

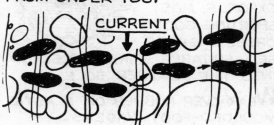

CURRENT

WADING PROBLEMS

STREAM
ANGLERS CAN
COVER MUCH MORE WATER WITH
LESS FATIGUE WHEN WADING
DOWNSTREAM WITH THE CURRENT
THAN UPSTREAM AGAINST IT.
IT'S NECESSARY TO BE CAUTIOUS
OF CURRENTS TOO STRONG TO
RETREAT AGAINST WHERE IT MAY
BECOME TOO DEEP FOR WADING.

NEW USERS OF HIGH TOP WADERS
SHOULD NOT BE OVERCONFIDENT
OF DEEP WATER BECAUSE IN
DEEPER WATER ONE'S BODY BE-
COMES MORE BUOYANT AND THE
FEET HAVE LESS TRACTION. HIP
HIGH IS <u>DEEP</u> IN FAST WATER!

271

APPROACH A POOL BY WADING SAFELY!

WITH SLIGHTLY BENT KNEES WORK UPSTREAM SIDEWISE.

← CURRENT

APPROACHING DEEPER POOLS FROM DOWNSTREAM SO THAT IF THE FOOTING BECOMES IN-SECURE, BACKTRACKING WILL BE EASIER WITH THE CURRENT THAN AGAINST IT. IF YOU SHOULD BE SWEPT OFF YOUR FEET__ THE CURRENT TAKES YOU TOWARD SHALLOW WATER INSTEAD OF HEAD OVER HEELS INTO DEEPER WATER!

← CURRENT

THE HEAD OF THE POOL IS USUALLY ITS DEEPEST END.

FIRST
AID...

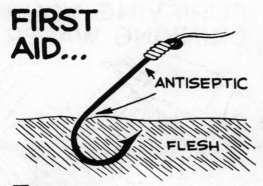

ANTISEPTIC

FLESH

TREATMENT FOR FISH HOOK
WOUND CAN BE SIMPLE!

DO NOT ATTEMPT TO PULL
IMBEDDED BARB OUT!

COVER EXPOSED PART OF
HOOK WITH ANTISEPTIC AND
THEN <u>PUSH</u> BARB ON
THROUGH.

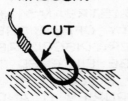

CUT

A SMART
FISHERMAN
CARRIES A
COMBINATION
ALL-PURPOSE
TOOL OR SET

OF CLIPPERS. THIS MAY BE
USED TO CLIP THE HOOK
SHANK.

NOW PULL THE OFFENDING
BARB OUT...
POINT FIRST!

273

PURIFYING YOUR DRINKING WATER...

WILDERNESS STREAMS AND LAKES USUALLY OFFER THE PUREST WATER. DISCOLORED WATER MAY BE FILTERED TO CLEAR IT AND BOILED FOR 15 MINUTES TO PURIFY IT AND THEN COOLED FOR DRINKING. ONE-HALF TEASPOON OF FRESH CHLORIDE OF LIME IN A PINT OF <u>ANY</u> WATER WILL PURIFY IT. AS A RULE, THE FARTHER THE WATER IS FROM HUMAN HABITATION, THE SAFER IT IS!

TIMELY INSECT TIPS

Flies and
mosquitoes
are quite
bothersome
unless a
breeze
keeps
them
away
or...

...You are prepared
with a repelling solution on
the exposed parts. Here are
2 inexpensive formulas to try.

① Mix: ½ oz. of each; citronella,
spirits of camphor, pennyroyal,
oil of cloves, oil of peppermint.
Add 5 oz. olive oil, shake well.

② Mix: 1 oz. spirits of camphor,
1 oz. citronella and ½ oz. oil
of cedar.

These formulas aren't ruinous
to a fly line's finish as some
commercial repellants are.

A drop of spirits of ammonia on
an insect bite relieves sting.

INDEX